THE SECRET HUN

GW00643825

Many British servicemen and women who
failed to return from the war against Nazi
Germany would have remained 'missing in
action' if officialdom had had its way. SAS
troops illegally shot as saboteurs under
Hitler's Commando Order and SOE agents
murdered in concentration camps were to be
forgotten in the euphoria that followed VE
Day.

But when the SAS and SOE were
disbanded after the war there were those
who felt their job was incomplete, that they
owed something to the men and women who
had lost their lives behind enemy lines. They
determined to discover the truth about their
missing comrades and bring to justice those
responsible for crimes.

Making use of the first official report on the
horrors of the Nazi concentration camps —
written as early as December 1944 but
suppressed by Allied headquarters — The
Secret Hunters set out to establish the fates
of the missing men and women.

Based on the personal testimony of
witnesses, on interviews with the hunters
themselves and using secret personal
papers and unpublished official documents,
THE SECRET HUNTERS is a powerful account
of painstaking detective work carried out by a
handful of people who cared about their
comrades . . . and a horrific indictment of
official inertia.

'An amazing story'   *Catholic Herald*

About the author

Anthony Kemp is forty-seven years old and grew up during the war. After school and National Service in the RAF, he worked in Germany for a number of years where he learnt the language and gained an interest in modern German history. He studied history at Oxford as a mature student, and since 1982 he has been employed by TVS as a researcher. He is the author of ten books on military subjects.

The Secret Hunters

Anthony Kemp

CORONET BOOKS
Hodder and Stoughton

British Library C.I.P.

Kemp, Anthony
  The secret hunters.
  1. War Criminals—Germany 2. World
War 1939–1945—Atrocities
  I. Title
  364.1'38'094   D804.G4

  ISBN 0 340 41901 6

Printed and bound in Great Britain
for Hodder and Stoughton
Paperbacks, a division of Hodder and
Stoughton Ltd., Mill Road,
Dunton Green, Sevenoaks, Kent
TN13 2YA.
(Editorial Office: 47 Bedford Square,
London WC1B 3DP) by
Cox & Wyman Ltd., Reading

Contents

Contents

List of illustrations

List of maps and diagrams

Foreword

Many people today imagine that the Nuremberg trials settled the fate of the Nazi war criminals, yet we regularly read in the press that another aged malefactor has been discovered in the depths of South America. Klaus Barbie still awaits trial in Montluc Prison in Lyons, and there was the recent controversy over the death of Dr Mengele in Brazil. Another popular misconception is that concentration camps were set up solely for the purpose of killing off the Jews of Europe. It is hardly known that millions of others found their way into those loathsome places and that among them were British civilians and service personnel – airmen, secret agents and airborne troops, sailors and commandos.

Today the camps are memorials, sanitised, equipped with toilets to cope with the streams of visitors through the well laid out museums. Imposing monuments designed by famous sculptors implore us, the post-war generation, to remember the victims, mostly anonymous, who were brought to these places to suffer and die in degradation. Figures become meaningless when considered in millions and so too are the photographs of the piles of discarded clothing, heaps of human hair and the stick-like bodies of those whose race, politics or religious beliefs did not tie in with those of their oppressors.

The obituaries of those millions have been written by others. This book is concerned with a small number of British and Allied service personnel who died on active service – not with honour in the front line, but through murder, alone and naked, contrary to any definition of natural justice and common humanity. It is also about their friends and comrades who, with scant encouragement from officialdom, set out to determine the truth about their deaths and bring those responsible to justice.

The television film, *The Secret Hunters*, on which this study is based, was made by Television South and I am most grateful to the company for granting me the facilities to expand on the film and to write down so much of the research material which we could not use. My thanks are due especially to Peter Williams, Head of Factual Programmes, and Martyn Lewis who presented it. It was he who gave me a shove in the right direction. I owe a great debt to Gordon Stevens who directed the film, for his forbearance and tolerance in the face of endless history lectures, and to the 'crew' who made it all possible.

Introduction

Wars since the beginning of this century have become much less than a personal 'blood & guts' affair, or so it seemed to many of us in the 1939-45 War. Bombs, artillery, tanks and attacks from the air all seemed so impersonal, with the antagonists rarely in sight. This lack of physical contact with the adversary meant that the impression carried by the majority about the Germans was only relayed to them secondhand.

It was different in those countries which were occupied as they experienced mass deportation or suffered reprisals, brought on by active resistance. To the people of Britain, however, deportation to staff-up armament factories or to build fortifications, although against International Convention, were understandable, as were severe penalties for resistance. It was not until nearly the end of the war that the exact nature of those penalties were disclosed.

Up to 1944 little evidence of brutality, let alone bestiality, was available; even the full extent of the deportation of Jews, while known about, was not generally appreciated. Then a strange thing happened – when the reports of war crimes really did begin to come in as the allies liberated Europe, neither the soldiers nor the politicians wanted to know. Only the French manfully tried to bring home the horrors that had been perpetrated. It is quite inexplicable why when evidence was available it was deliberately suppressed by British and Americans alike.

Only when camps like Belsen were reached was there an official outcry, in spite of the facts being known a good six months before. A negative attitude prevailed right until VE-Day and the excuse given was that exposure of the truth might prejudice the safety of our prisoners of war. People just did not want to know; soldiers and politicians alike hesitated at opening doors to horrors even more devastating than fighting and bombing had inflicted on the British people.

It was in such an atmosphere that lip service was paid in pursuing the perpetrators of war crimes, with pressure brought by the French and by all the countries in Europe that had been occupied. The French, the Dutch, the Danes and the Norwegians, all were diligent in looking for those responsible. Not so the British; the organisation was there but neither the will nor the enthusiasm; so it is not surprising that the story that this book tells is almost unique.

Two distinct attitudes towards war crimes were forming, by those who were directly exposed to their effects and by those who had merely heard of them secondhand.

The official British and US war crimes teams and the allied administration were all soldiers, most of whom had experienced conventional war with all its dangers but who had little knowledge of war crimes. To them their responsibility was a job of work which might delay their demobilisation. Only the lawyers and the Judge Advocate General's department who had to study the evidence really appreciated the horrors which were coming to light.

This story is basically one of two dedicated people united in a passionate loyalty to their comrades in arms, both highly intelligent and motivated by a very full understanding of what had happened in occupied Europe.

It was fortuitous for me that I fitted in and that the cooperation between Bill, Vera and myself worked so well, because by chance all had common ground and we were able to feed on each other's enthusiasm. Until I landed in France my only experience of war had been in a battered convoy at sea and in North Africa, where much of the time action had been sporadic and so almost unrealistic. But then when my responsibilities took me into premises which had been occupied by the Gestapo and into the first concentration camp which we liberated. This had an immediate and profound effect on me – from then on every German seemed evil and I was seized with that same sense of dedication that motivated both Bill Barkworth and Vera Atkins.

To me it is so sad that Bill is dead, only months before his work is achieving public recognition. He was a man of great education and intellect, capable of much ingenuity in pursuit of his objectives – ruthless in his singlemindedness but very fair in his treatment of others, even though they were suspected of unbelievable atrocities.

Vera Atkins had the same dedication, the same ability for penetrative thinking as Barkworth. She was like a mother who had lost her children for lost indeed they were, and their end inspired us all with a strong desire for revenge.

It was all so long ago, not many are living who remember those days as well as we do. I wonder that our memories survive since, as one grows older, the mind tries to jettison or stifle the unpleasant recollections. Time has helped to make me realise that I should not have hated all Germans, but only those whose baser instincts got the upper hand.

I have sometimes wondered if the chase should still go on for beasts like Mengele and Barbie and I have come to a very definite conclusion that such monsters must be tracked down and their story re-told. In this way the lessons for the future will not be forgotten. Luckily we have the ability of the media to remind and expose, let us hope that they will continue to watch for any recurrence in the conflicts of today.

Prince Yurka Galitzine

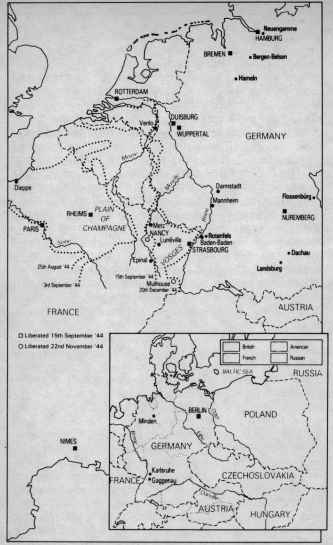

The Allied advance towards the Rhine and (inset) the post-war division of
Germany. The Secret Hunters, operating from a base at Gaggenau, ranged
over the British, French and American zones in their search for evidence of
crimes against their comrades.

16

1

A reason to hunt

The International Military Tribunal which sat at Nuremberg
was set up by the victorious Allies, with its judges drawn from
America, Britain, Russia and France. The Tribunal's high-
flown purpose was to make the Nazi leaders answer for their
actions, not only during the course of hostilities but dating
back to their seizure of power in 1933. The most wanted men
– Hitler, Himmler and Goebbels – had committed suicide,
while Martin Bormann was tried in his absence. Those in the
dock, perhaps with the exception of Göring, were the 'second
eleven' of the Nazi hierarchy, those who had obeyed orders to
execute, to pull triggers and to open the doors of the gas
chambers and furnaces. The four counts on which the defendants at Nuremberg were indicted were: conspiracy to wage
aggressive war; crimes against peace; war crimes; and crimes
against humanity.

The story of the Nuremberg Tribunal has been dealt with in
a number of studies. What concerns *The Secret Hunters* is the
British attitude to war crimes – acts committed against members of the armed forces or civilians of one of the belligerent
powers, contrary to the laws and usages of war.

The 'atrocity' story first surfaced in the First World War, to
be exploited by both sides as propaganda. The beastly Hun
raped Belgian nuns and slaughtered babies wholesale. It is
quite clear that war crimes were committed and it is unlikely
that the Germans had a total monopoly of beastliness. The
Armistice in 1918 left Germany intact as a sovereign state, but
the Allies reserved the right to try German citizens for violation of the laws and customs of war, as a provision of the
Treaty of Versailles. Germany refused to hand over the
wanted men and in a compromise it was agreed that they
themselves would try the accused. The result was a series of
trials that ended in derisory sentences passed on the few
found guilty and a vast wave of popular sympathy for the
'heroes'.

The essential nastiness of National Socialism was certainly apparent during the 1930s, but as appeasement was the order of the day there was no official encouragement to harp on the fact. The Italians in Abyssinia and the horrors of the Spanish Civil War, however, received ample coverage and were exploited by those on the receiving end. When the Second World War broke out, the general assumption was that it would end with Germany forced into seeking an armistice under an alternative government once the Nazi regime had been toppled from within. In 1939 nobody envisaged total defeat and occupation of enemy territory.

Soon after the occupation of Poland, atrocity stories began to surface and were given some press coverage, but tended to be dismissed as exaggerated. It has to be admitted that passive anti-semitism was widespread in Britain at the time among the governing classes, and anyway the Foreign Office could not envisage taking on responsibility for prosecuting Germans for crimes committed in a foreign country. It was felt that a commitment to hunt down and try thousands of guilty Germans would be quite impossible to carry out. Only Churchill fostered the idea of eventual retribution, much to the horror of the Foreign Office whose officials sought throughout the war to limit any public implication of a postwar witch hunt.

In 1941 the German invasion of Russia resulted in a new wave of horror reports and daily broadcasts over Moscow Radio detailing German crimes, which could easily be dismissed as propaganda. The very real stories that started to come in from the Far East in the spring of 1942, however, could not so easily be shrugged off, for they concerned British servicemen and civilians captured by the Japanese. In addition, as an act of revenge for the assassination of Heydrich in Prague, the village of Lidice was razed to the ground and its entire population either shot or deported. In August, the first intimation of the planned 'final solution of the Jewish question' surfaced in London and Washington but was simply disbelieved. To herd the Jews into ghettos was considered possible but the murder of millions could not be envisaged.

The first definitive statement by the Allies on the subject of punishment for war crimes was not issued until November

1943 in Moscow: those responsible for atrocities were to be sent back to the countries in which their crimes had been committed, for punishment. At the same time, the grandly titled United Nations War Crimes Commission (UNWCC) held its first meeting. As far as Washington and London were concerned, too much fuss about war crimes might stir the Germans into taking reprisals against Allied prisoners of war. The UNWCC was left to operate in a vacuum having been set up as a sop to public opinion, and it was not until May 1944 that the Foreign Office and the War Office agreed to hand over their own lists of war criminals. The War Office had restricted their interest to crimes against British service personnel and by that date had some indications of those responsible for two massacres in 1940, at Le Paradis and Wormhoudt during the retreat to Dunkirk. In August 1944, the Commission had to admit that they had collected only 184 names and had not included Hitler. This provoked considerable criticism in the press but nothing was done to alter official unwillingness.

In the early summer of 1944 information was received that fifty RAF officers, who were among those who escaped from Stalag Luft III at Sagan via a tunnel, had been shot by the Gestapo. Yet when the Allies landed in Normandy on 6 June there was no clear policy at Eisenhower's headquarters for dealing with war crimes. As country after country was liberated more and more evidence of crimes came to light but it was not until October 1944 that an embryo investigation unit was authorised at Supreme Headquarters Allied Expeditionary Force (SHAEF). It was concerned, however, only with crimes committed against Allied nationals after D-Day. While the Americans had committed themselves to investigating crimes dating back to 1933, in Britain the War Office was aghast at the prospect. As a result, other than holding meetings in an attempt to delay matters, nothing concrete was done until the liberation of Bergen-Belsen on 15 April 1945 forced the government to set up an official War Crimes Investigation Unit.

Official indifference to the fate of millions – not only Jews but also Gypsies, Jehovah's Witnesses, political opponents of the Nazi regime and even homosexuals – was such that even in

May 1945 there was still no clear war crimes policy, in spite of the vast numbers of Germans already in captivity. The attitude towards the British servicemen and women who had played their part in the defeat of Germany was that they had simply failed to return. The indignation that should have been felt was missing. To discover their fates and to bring to justice the people who had been responsible for crimes against them was, all too often, left to private initiative.

2

The Commando Order

The Special Air Service Regiment (SAS) evolved in the Western Desert campaigns during 1941. Its basic purpose was to harry German communications and to create havoc behind German lines. Although on many occasions SAS units co-operated with local partisans and resistance units in Greece, Italy and France for example, its members were always part of the properly constituted armed forces of Britain. As such they operated in uniform, carried service identity tags and were entitled to the protection afforded to combatants by various international agreements such as the Geneva Convention. The SAS operated as far afield as Norway, North Africa and the Far East, as well as in Europe, conducting raids with from as few as three men up to battalion level operations. Its members were specially chosen not only for their fighting qualities but also for their intelligence and initiative, and many of the early recruits came from the ranks of the Commandos. They were not a collection of thugs and guerillas, but rather a disparate grouping of highly efficient soldiers often imbued with a certain intellectual detachment about the profession of arms. Their individual exploits are worthy of a whole series of books but so far only the outlines of their activities have been made public.

It is an internationally accepted right of any nation at war to operate anywhere in enemy territory. Paragraph 45 of Chapter 30 of the *Manual of Militiary Law* applicable during the war years clearly stated: 'Train wrecking and setting on fire camps and military depots are legitimate means of injuring the enemy when carried out by members of the Armed Forces.'

In the early stages of the war, the German armed forces made extensive use of airborne and land-based raiding parties. During the May/June campaign in France and the Low Countries in 1940, there was the spectacular glider landing on top of the Belgian fort of Eben Emäel, a seaplane landing on the Maas at Rotterdam, and clandestine attacks on the Maas bridges at Venlo and Gennep. The purpose of such operations was to capture vital communications links to speed the advance of the main army units.*.

In August 1941, Dr Waltzog of the Legal Department of the German High Command stated that:

At the beginning of this war the opinion was held abroad that German parachutists were not legal combatants but *franc tireurs* or spies. This is incorrect. Parachute units are part of the German Armed Forces and belong to the Luftwaffe. Members of these units are legal combatants and undertake legitimate military tasks.

Their combatant status is the same whether they are employed at the front or behind it. It is equally the same whether they are dropped in groups or singly. One should compare them with a scout. As soldiers they wear the uniform given to them and which was made known to the enemy.

Nevertheless, Hitler regarded enemy raids on territory occupied by his forces as a form of personal insult. On 7 October 1942 a statement was issued with the daily Wehrmacht communiqué: 'In future all terrorist and sabotage troops of the British and their accomplices who conduct themselves not as soldiers but as bandits will be treated as such by German troops and will be ruthlessly killed in action wherever they may appear.'

On 17 October a newspaper article was published detailing alleged breaches of international law by the Allies. The following day the so-called Commando Order was issued which provided that members of raiding parties were to be killed in combat, shot after interrogation, or handed over to the security service (Sicherheitsdienst or SD) of the SS. It is reckoned that this order cost the lives of some 250 Allied servicemen

---

*Both the Germans and Italians continued to use parachute- and glider-landed troops. In 1944 midget submarines and battle swimmers were involved in attacks on Allied shipping and against bridges in Normandy and Holland. In December 1944, Otto Skorzeny used airborne troops to liberate Mussolini and infiltrated commandos dressed as Americans behind enemy lines during the Ardennes offensive, those captured by the Americans in US uniform were justifiably executed.

and it was even used at times against air force crews who had been shot down and captured.

The SAS knew nothing about the secret Commando Order until the spring of 1944 when they received a report from Lieutenant Quentin 'Jimmy' Hughes of 2 SAS, stationed in Italy. Hughes was one of six parachutists of 2 SAS selected to take part in Operation Pomegranate whose purpose was to destroy German reconnaissance aircraft at San Egido near Perugia. On 12 January 1944 they were dropped by a United States C-47 but while making their way towards the airfield the party was split up. The two officers, Major Widdrington and Lieutenant Hughes, reached the target on the night of 17/18 January and succeeded in placing Lewes bombs on the seven aircraft they found there. Unfortunately, while one of the bombs was being disarmed, it exploded, killing the major and severely wounding Hughes. Deafened and blinded, Hughes was captured, given first aid and taken to the Policlinico at Perugia where he received excellent treatment.

It was only after he started to recover that Hughes realised that he was being held as a political prisoner and the vexed question of uniform came up. He had jumped wearing an old battledress and a balaclava helmet. For the raid he wore plimsolls, leaving his boots in a rucksack some way away from the target. During interrogation Hughes was told that when recovered he would be handed over to the Gestapo to be shot as a saboteur.

The doctor in charge of the hospital, Hans Gunter Sontgerath, befriended Hughes, as did Major Gerhard Schacht, a patient in the next room. Schacht was a General Staff officer who had taken part in the glider drop on Eben Emäel and other special operations. As Hughes began to regain his sight the two Germans decided to try to avoid having to hand him over to the Gestapo. Fortunately Schacht had some influence with Kesselring, the German Commander-in-Chief in Italy, and literally at the last minute had Hughes's papers amended to show he was a prisoner of war. Armed with this they were able to put him on a train for the main prisoner clearing camp at Mantua.

Realising, however, that the arm of the Gestapo was a long one, the only partially recovered Hughes managed to escape from the train with an American and make his way to the British lines. The tale he brought back to his regiment about parachutists being automatically shot was included in a memorandum known as 'The Hughes Report' which was passed to HQ 1 Airborne Corps, as by that time the unit was in England preparing for the Normandy landings. In an official report issued after the war, Major E.W. Barkworth, Intelligence Officer of 2 SAS, commented on how Hughes's experience was ignored:

Hughes' case was dismissed as mere interrogation technique, and reference to other men of the Regiment who had neither returned, nor had been reported as casualties, was explained away by the fact that the enemy probably wished to keep us in the dark about the success of operations...

It was not until the dead bodies of murdered prisoners had been found in France and a copy of the Commando Order in Italy in the Autumn of 1944 that these actions of the Germans were taken seriously; even then, it was only in March 1945 that Eisenhower (the Allied Supreme Commander) made a wireless proclamation.

Thus it was with only a vague intimation of their likely fate that SAS units took part in a series of clandestine but legitimate operations after D-Day in June 1944.

3

Operation Loyton

The post D-Day stalemate in Normandy was broken at the end of July 1944 and, after the great round-up in the Falaise pocket, the Allies were at the Seine on 15 August. The German forces in the West had suffered a crushing defeat. The Third US, commanded by General George S. Patton, swept across Northern France, liberating Rheims and Epinal towards the end of August. Paris fell on 24 August and the heady pursuit into Belgium and across the flat plain of Champagne went ahead with all the dash of old fashioned cavalry operations. Allied sights were fixed on the Rhine and all the talk was about the war being over by Christmas.

The speed of the American advance, combined with Allied optimism, led to the decision to drop a party of SAS troops into the Vosges to interrupt German communications during the assumed retreat and to stiffen the relatively untrained Resistance fighters. Equipped with long-range jeeps,* about one hundred members of the regiment were to be dropped. The operation was codenamed 'Loyton'.

Beyond the Moselle rise the wooded slopes of the Vosges mountains, barring the way to the Rhine valley and the ancient imperial city of Strasbourg. Although not high in the Alpine sense, the Vosges are crossed by only a few passes suitable for heavy traffic and the terrain is broken by deep ravines, tumbling streams and thick forests, easily defended by a determined enemy. Such problems were further complicated by ethnic difficulties as Lorraine's chequered history had led to divided loyalties. The area up to the Rhine was finally incorporated into France by Louis XIV towards the end of the seventeenth century, although the language was

*Fitted with extra fuel tanks, the jeeps had a range of up to 700 miles; the main armament consisted of twin Vickers .303 machine guns mounted front and rear. In addition they could be fitted with mortars and could tow small anti-tank guns.

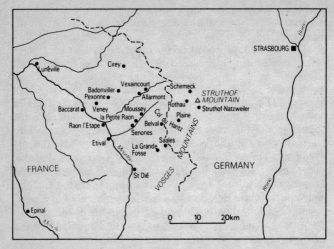

Operation Loyton, August to October 1944. The broken line indicates the
1940 to 1944 frontier between France and Germany.

Germanic. As a result of the Franco-Prussian War in 1870 the provinces of Alsace and Lorraine were declared to be part of Germany and the new frontier ran along the crest of the Vosges – one side German and the other French. France went to war in 1914 with the avowed intention of regaining the lost provinces. It took them four years and millions of dead and maimed but the tricolour waved once more over Metz and Strasbourg. In 1940 the Germans expelled the disorganised French troops in a matter of days and Alsace and Lorraine were reincorporated into the Reich – not occupied like other parts of France.

Thus in 1944 the area in which the SAS was to operate was divided by an artificial frontier and inhabited by people who spoke a German dialect. On one side of the border were citizens of Hitler's Reich and on the other they were French, living discontentedly under the oppression of an occupying power. The majority regarded themselves as French and were intensely patriotic; by August 1944 the Maquis was active in harassing German convoys. Others, however, felt themselves to be German and did all they could to aid and abet the authorities.

The terrain in which the SAS were to drop was ideal for concealment and ambushes, as the enemy was confined to the few available roads. East of Nancy and Lunéville there were few towns of any size and the villages consisted of single streets of houses straggling along the valleys. In the woods themselves, the only habitations were isolated foresters' huts and the occasional lonely farm.

At the beginning of the operation, the German front line was some hundred miles to the west but in fairly disorganised retreat. The enemy was under additional pressure from the American and French units which had landed in the south of France on 15 August and were moving up towards the Vosges. In headlong flight were the hordes of rear echelon formations – signals and stores depots, Luftwaffe ground crews, mobile blacksmith companies, complete field hospitals, and all the apparatus of repression – whose only aim was to get themselves back across the Rhine. As the Allies advanced, the first to leave the scene of their crimes were various police and Gestapo formations.

The German machinery of repression was organised from Berlin by the Reich Security Headquarters (RHSA), commanded by Ernst Kaltenbrünner but controlled ultimately by Himmler. Both Germany and the occupied territories were divided up into areas under a local Commander of the Security Police (BDS). Two of these, BDS Alsace and BDS France, were to play a significant part in Operation Loyton.

BDS Alsace was located in Strasbourg at 10 Rue d'Alsace and was commanded by Dr Isselhorst, a lawyer who had joined the Gestapo in 1935. His deputy was Obersturmbannführer Wilhelm Schneider whom Isselhorst, when interrogated in 1945 by the SAS investigators, described as a 'drunken old fool'. Schneider was a one-time merchant captain, characterised after the war as having been 'pompous, ineffective and fond of drink'.

Within the area of BDS Alsace there were two camps, one of which was the only concentration camp on French soil, known as Struthof-Natzweiler. The other was the Sicherungslager (Security Camp) of Schirmeck which included a number of subsidiary camps on the other side of the Rhine in Germany.

BDS France was originally housed in Paris where its staff was responsible both for the deportation to the Polish extermination camps of the Jewish population and the war against the Resistance. In mid-August of 1944 the headquarters was withdrawn from Paris to Nancy where it remained for about a month before retreating to Germany in the face of the Allied advance.

BDS Alsace and France had a number of units of agents in the field, *Einsatzkommandos*, who were responsible for coping with the Maquis and other local opposition. A number of these groups had moved into the area in early August having been displaced from their previous operating grounds and were destined to take the responsibility for the murder of SAS prisoners of war as well as a number of Allied airmen who fell into their hands.

Kommando Schöner, with an approximate strength of thirty including a number of men from the Karlsruhe Gestapo, was originally based at Raon l'Etape. Schöner himself ordered a precipitate retreat from that town on 8

September, for which he was arrested and disgraced.

Kommando Wenger moved into the area from Paris in August and was part of BDS France. With a total strength of some ninety officers and men, the unit was based at various places in the immediate area of the SAS operation. Its members were to be directly implicated in a number of murders. Several French traitors were attached to the unit, as was a guard company of Azerbaijans and other oriental Russians.

Kommando Retzek was originally based in Cannes and was mainly made up of French Milice, including a number of Arabs. Known as a *Jagdkommando*, it operated over a fairly wide area based initially at Nancy, then at Baccarat and Celles sur Plaine.

Kommando zbV 6 Dr Ernst retreated into the Vosges from Angers on the Loire and set up a base at St Dié in early September 1944, later moving to Saales. The unit included a group of about twenty French civilians. While at Angers, the Kommando was implicated in the murder of a number of men from 1 SAS who were in that area after D-Day.

In addition, there were several smaller Gestapo and police units operating in the Vosges as well as an Abwehr (counter-intelligence) section known as Gruppe Kieffer. Inevitably too, the Wehrmacht became involved in police actions against the Maquis. The area military command was in Strasbourg under General Vaterrodt, who sent units to assist the Gestapo in rounding up partisans. The ground troops fighting the main battle against the Allied forces were in a state of flux at the end of August as they frantically tried to reorganise after the headlong retreat from France. Hitler, in his determination to hold on to as much of France as possible, had ordered a new line of fortifications to be hastily prepared. This line ran along the forward slopes of the Vosges and consisted of little more than ill-prepared trenches and anti-tank ditches. The front line became more stable along the line of the Moselle through Nancy at the beginning of September, held by a number of scratch divisions with their lines of communication running back through the mountains.

The advance party of fifteen SAS men dropped on the night of 12/13 August 1944 near La Petite Raon, accompanied by a Jedburgh team from Special Forces whose mission was to

son with the French. This section consisted of
.ough and Barreaux and Sergeant Seymour. The
.istance was established in the hills around the village
.ssey and was called the Groupe Mobile d'Alsace
(.). Loosely attached was 1 Regiment de Chasseurs
Vosgiennes FFI (Forces Françaises de l'Intérieur). It is not
clear exactly how many French people were under arms in the
area but the total ran into several hundreds, many of them
young who had fled into the mountains to avoid deportation
to Germany for forced labour. One of the volunteers was a
seventeen-year-old student named Roger Souchal, now a
well-known lawyer in Nancy.

With the first drop was a small unit of 'Phantom' signals
brigade, responsible for communications to Britain, commanded by Captain John Hislop whose first operation was
Loyton. In his book *Anything but a Soldier* he recorded:

By now the Germans were very much alive to our presence and
began to move troops into our areas. We had to keep on the move
continually. Every now and then the Germans would find our camp
and move into attack, but always we got away. The forests of the
area were a great boon, since they made it difficult for the Germans
to find us and, having done so, to pin us down. They did not seem
anxious to stray far from the tracks and never ventured into the
woods after dark.

Four men from the advance party were taken prisoner.
Sergeant Seymour sprained his ankle as a result of the drop
and was soon captured. Sergeants Lodge and Davis and Private Hall became separated and were captured between the
17 and 20 August.

By the night of 1/2 September the advance party had managed to create a suitable base and the first of the main groups,
commanded by Lieutenent Colonel Brian Franks, together
with jeeps and stores, dropped into a reception committee
near Veney. The rest of the unit followed a week later into a
dropping zone near Pexonne. This coincided with the stiffen-
ing of the German front line some fifteen miles to the west of
the operational area and the American halt caused by fuel
shortage. Patton's two corps, XX and XII, were closing up
along the line of the Meuse when they stalled for lack of fuel.

All supplies were still having to be landed over the open beaches in Normandy and it was not until the 5th that the advance towards the Moselle could be resumed. From there they headed into country totally unsuitable for wide-ranging armoured warfare and devoid of airfields from which fighter-bombers could operate.

The Germans decided to mount a series of punitive sweeps starting on 1 September in the general area of the Vosges under the code name Operation *Waldfest* I (*Waldfest* literally means a woodland party). Schneider of BDS Alsace was placed in command of *Waldfest*, operating from an office set up at the Schirmeck camp. He was assisted by Hauptsturm-führer Julius Gehrum, said to be even more fond of drink than his boss, and a police officer, Uhring.

The scene was set for a planned campaign of attrition. While the Germans were entitled to clear up their rear areas, and to shoot Frenchmen found in civilian clothes as partisans, the murder of members of the British regular forces captured in uniform was unjustifiable and was to lead to those responsible standing trial for their actions.

Three men on the second main SAS unit drop became separated and one of them, Private Elliott, broke his thigh. They hid out in a farm until captured on 16 September. Meanwhile, it was decided to transfer the main body to the Moussey area where it was felt that there would be less opposition. The young Roger Souchal had been enrolled as interpreter for Colonel Franks and also functioned as a guide. Another staunch local ally was the forester Albert Freine. It soon became obvious that the local Maquis was riddled with informers and reluctantly the decision had to be made to have as little contact as possible with the larger units.

Day after day the patrols sallied out in their jeeps, shooting up convoys, mining roads and demolishing bridges, but they suffered the inevitable losses. What had been envisaged as a ten-day venture became a protracted operation as the Americans made slow headway towards the hills. It was not until 15 September that Nancy fell to the 35th Infantry Division and US tanks rolled towards Lunéville. The tiny group of para-chutists found themselves operating against the communications of General Manteuffel's Fifth Panzer Army which had

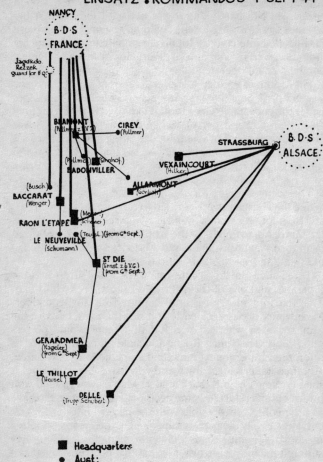

EINSATZ · KOMMANDOS · I · SEPT · 44

NANCY
B·D·S
FRANCE

Jagdkdo
Reizek
guard for H Q:

BLAMONT
(Pullmelz, V.?)

CIREY
(Pullmer)

STRASSBURG

B·D·S
ALSACE

VEXAINCOURT
(Hilker)

(Pullmer) (Sinohof.)
BADONVILLER

ALLAIMONT
(Gorloff)

(Busch)
BACCARAT
(Wenger)

(Meler,
Schaner.)
RAON L'ETAPE

(Teusel.) (from 6ª Sept.)
LE NEUVEVILLE
(Schumann)

ST DIE
(Ernst z.b.V.G.)
(from 6ª Sept.)

GERARDMEA
(Nageler)
(from 6ª Sept)

LE THILLOT
(Heusel)

DELLE
(Trupp Schubert)

■ Headquarters
● Aust:

The organisation behind Operation *Waldfest* I. BDS Alsace and France had a number of units of agents, *Einsatzkommandos*, operating against the SAS in the Vosges area. The diagram is one of six showing the activities of the units included in Major Barkworth's detailed report on 'Missing Parachutists'.

32

been rushed south from Belgium in a bid to stop Patton. But the great counter-attack fizzled out after two days of action around Lunéville and a grim war of attrition was fought until the end of September when a general lull was imposed on both sides.*

But for the war it is unlikely that anyone outside the immediate locality would ever have heard of Moussey. Tucked away from the main road that leads across the Vosges between Lunéville and Strasbourg via the Col du Hantz, it straggles along the valley forged by a small mountain stream. Before the war the population was some 1,130, making a modest living from forestry, subsistence agriculture and a textile factory. There was a church, a Mairie, a few shops and cafés, and most of the houses were owned by the textile concern which was a patriarchal family business. The village was on the French side of the post-1870 frontier, situated only a few miles to the east.

Christopher Sykes, the historian, served as an officer in the SAS and took part in Operation Loyton. He wrote in an article for the regimental magazine:

We depended on the people of Moussey for many of the necessities of life, and for help of every kind. They gave us everything we asked for and more. They were the staunchest of allies and in manifestly bad times, for with the holdup of the American Army and continued German reinforcements along the river Meurthe a few miles to the west, our difficulties increased daily. It was a nightmare time but throughout it the civilian population was in far greater danger than we were. We could move rapidly from place to place but, except for a few of the men, the civilians could not and if they did, perforce left hostages behind.

During the move to the Moussey area, a further eight men were captured after they had been spotted by a French informer who brought in a Gestapo detachment to the farm where they were hiding. More jeeps were parachuted in but the onset of bad weather made supply drops a hazardous business in such difficult country and in the presence of an active

*For a detailed account of the fighting in Lorraine that Autumn, see Anthony Kemp, *The Unknown Battle, Metz 1944*, Leo Cooper, London, and Stein and Day, New York, 1980.

opposition. At the beginning of October, Colonel Franks was ordered to leave with the main body of the unit. As they fought their way through to the American lines, several more men were captured.

When the main body departed, a rear party was left to wait for Sergeant Neville and two men who were away on a patrol near the Col du Hantz. Roger Souchal, known as 'Armand', was expressly asked by Franks to stay with them. On 5 October they were surrounded by a force of Germans, probably from an armoured unit. The battle raged for four hours before lack of ammunition forced them to surrender. All were captured by the Wehrmacht troops and were handed over to *Kommando* zbV 6 Dr Ernst. All the British were shot. Only the Frenchman, Roger Souchal, survived.

Souchal tried to persuade his captors that he was a French Canadian member of the SAS but when the *Einsatzkommando* moved its headquarters to Maison Barthelmy in Saales a French woman working there denounced him as a member of the Maquis. At the age of seventeen he was taken to a concentration camp. After the war he was awarded the King's Medal. The citation stated:

Between the 31 August and 5 October 1944, Monsieur Roger Souchal ... served as courier and guide to a detachment of SAS in the Vosges. Between 19 and 21 September he took part in ambushes against German convoys ... His conduct during the course of these operations was exemplary and the manner in which he employed his knowledge of the locality was of vital importance to the SAS detachments whereby an error in the choice of route could have cost the life of the detachment. In addition he assisted at five parachute drops and on not less than ten occasions visited houses in the locality to obtain provisions ... Monsieur Souchal never ceased to prove his great courage and evident determination in carrying out his tasks in assisting the SAS detachment – work which he undertook voluntarily and in full knowledge of the risks involved.

The support given by the local people to the small British presence was to cost them dearly. In a swoop on Moussey on 18 August the Germans had arrested a number of men. On 24 September they returned to round up the entire male population in the square. In vain the courageous parish priest, Abbé

Gassmann, offered his life in exchange for his parishioners. The Germans told him that his place was to stay with the women. The men were marched off to the nearby Château Belval where they joined others from neighbouring villages and towns, *en route* for concentration camps – Struthof-Natzweiler, Dachau, Belsen, and the extermination camp at Auschwitz. Of the 256 taken from Moussey, 144 did not return to their quiet valley. Senones had 350 deported, of whom 235 died, and La Petite Raon lost 128 out of 193 deportees. Twenty-nine Frenchmen were shot out of hand and three small villages were burnt to the ground. This put a temporary stop to Maquis activity in the area but the tide of war rolled on towards the Rhine – within two months Moussey was French once again.

Colonel Franks led the remaining members of his detachment back to England, to their base at Wivenhoe, near Colchester. He left behind thirty-one men who remained unaccounted for. Operation Loyton had taken a heavy toll.

4

The first official document

The Hughes report had given the SAS intelligence team at Wivenhoe an inkling of the possible fate of some of their men who were listed as 'missing' during Operation Loyton, as well as on other missions in occupied Europe. They knew nothing, however, about the German revenge on the people of Moussey and the deportations to concentration camps. Indeed, few people had any notion about the camps other than that they were centres for the 'concentration' of critics of the Nazi regime. There had been hints about the destiny of European Jewry but these were largely dismissed as Jewish propaganda.

On 15 August 1944 a combined American and French Army Group landed on the Mediterranean coast of France in Operation Dragoon. Their mission was to push north, clear the southern part of France and ultimately join with Eisenhower's armies for the combined advance into Germany. Their route was to take them towards the Vosges and on to the Rhine at Strasbourg.

On that same morning, a small Allied Combat Propaganda Team landed at St Tropez, then an unknown village, and made its way inland. The team's mission was to gather political intelligence for the Political Warfare Department of SHAEF. One of its members was the 21-year-old Captain Yurka Galitzine, a Russian prince with an English mother.

Galitzine was immediately drafted into a T-Force of three officers, one French, one American and one British, whose job was to report in detail on what the retreating German army left behind. Galitzine's first confrontation with the realities of Nazi occupation came in Nice where his team visited the Gestapo headquarters. To this day he remembers his first experience of 'what the Germans were like':

There were eleven bodies in the cellar, and one of them was the daughter of the mayor, Elaine Valiano, and I was horrified. She was about six or seven months gone with child and had been raped after death. I couldn't believe it. I just couldn't believe that people could behave like that.

At the end of November, the Combat Propaganda Team was in Alsace on the day Strasbourg was liberated. The entire Gestapo records for south-eastern France were captured in the city. These were to prove extremely useful to the Secret Hunters.

Nothing, however, could have prepared Captain Galitzine for what he was to discover on a lonely hilltop in the Vosges mountains. The remains of the concentration camp known as Struthof-Natzweiler had been liberated on 22 November by French troops operating with the US Seventh Army. 'I was briefed to go there,' Galitzine recalls, 'because I was told there was a concentration camp. We didn't know what that meant – being young and sort of only thinking about orthodox war, you know, and people just shooting each other.'

One early December morning Galitzine set off in a jeep with a group of French and American officers:

It was rather like a sort of tourist trip to start because it was so beautiful, just seeing the woods and the mountains. We didn't really know what to expect. I mean I had heard that there was a camp up there and I imagined it was going to be sort of either a tented camp or rather like a barracks. And when we arrived there the first thing that really hit one was the smell, which in fact you could tell quite a long way before you got to the camp. I suppose the best description is almost like a knacker's yard – a sort of deserted knacker's yard with coffins lying about and broken urns with human ashes lying around, piles of filthy clothes which smelt to high heaven.

With the Allies only eighty miles away, the camp had been evacuated on 4 September 1944 and most of the prisoners had been deported across the Rhine. After its liberation by French troops on 22 November there remained just a handful of prisoners from the nearby aircraft engine factory: 'A few rather dazed chaps,' Galitzine recalls, 'in striped suits wandering around – not very many of them. The most active ones had in fact actually got out and gone off to villages to try and get themselves cleaned up.' The team managed to track down eighteen witnesses to crimes committed at the camp. Galitzine heard a rumour that there had been British inmates and, to his surprise, he found detailed records of the camp in the administration block.

With the war only a few miles away, he left the Americans hunting for souvenirs and headed back to Strasbourg. A few weeks later, however, he returned on his own initiative to write a report on the camp and to investigate the fate of the possible British prisoners.* This report, 'based on personal investigation in the area in December 1944' is the first official document to describe the horror of a Nazi concentration camp. The ten closely typewritten pages present a grim picture of systematic executions by shooting, hanging and gassing, medical experiments carried out on live prisoners and starvation rations. A list of twenty-two 'German War Criminals in the Struthof affair' was attached to the report, the names of a handful of the SS men who had tortured, shot and brutalised thousands of prisoners.

Two of the eighteen witnesses had had continuous access to camp information. Ernst Krenzer, a local civil engineer, had worked in the stone quarries and had drawn up plans for the construction of a camp 'on the summit of the Struthof hill'. M. Nicole was a foreman employed by the firm of stonemasons contracted by the Germans to supervise quarry work. Their testimony enabled Galitzine to establish that the camp's original purpose had been to provide red Alsatian granite 'to face the "Party" buildings in Nuremberg'.

During the spring of 1941, work started not only on the quarry but also on building a road up the hill. Galitzine's report continues:

Suddenly without any warning one day in April several German military trucks trought 150 civilian prisoners up to the Hotel Struthof (closed some while before), where they were packed under guard and set to work. All the inhabitants of nearby farms and houses on the mountain were turned out and it became a restricted area . . .

---

*See Appendices A, B, C and D.

The numbers of the prisoners gradually increased and apparently at the same time the plans of the Germans became greatly enlarged in scope.

By the beginning of 1943 the camp on the summit of Struthof hill consisted of a military barracks for the SS guards and a wired-off area for the prisoners:

The prisoners' area was built in a clearing on an exposed slope of the mountain with a very beautiful view which was little compensated by the bitter cold climate at that altitude (3000 metres). It consisted of 15 barrack huts built in three rows of five on 'terraces' out of the mountain side. The whole compound was surrounded by a double wire fence with guard posts at intervals and through the wires ran a high voltage current.

When enough stone had been quarried, the prisoners were used as slave labour in the Junkers aircraft factory which was set up on the ledge formed by the excavations. From camp records, Galitzine discovered the Nazi plan:

They decided to use the camp as a holding centre for the distribution of prisoners to any government enterprise which needed manual labour with the idea of 'working the prisoners to death'. When a batch were so exhausted that they could work no more or had succumbed to some disease such as 'T.B.' or typhus, they were sent back to Struthof to be put out of their misery and a new batch was sent up to replace them. The areas 'serviced' by the camp appear to have been Alsace, Baden, Hesse and occasionally Lorraine.

Although the camp at Struthof itself never held more than 6,000-7,000 prisoners at a time, many thousands passed through its hands. On the work book of the camp in 1944 there were some 31 places listed involving at one moment 24,000 persons.

The camp records also revealed that the prisoners, at the outset mostly German political prisoners and Russians, came from Luxembourg, Holland, Belgium, Norway and Czechoslavakia. 'Later came Greek, Italian and Yugoslav partisans.' The first 'batch' of French were 'mainly curés and gendarmes'. The first Poles to be brought in 'were a whole village from near Lubin one night in 1942. Many of them were suffering from typhus.'

All the prisoners were classified under one of eight groups, Galitzine reported. The group signs were: 'Felon, Criminal, Political (military), Homosexuals, Political, Forced-labour dodgers, Bible forgers and Jews.' Galitzine added:

Certain prisoners who were considered more dangerous or who had attempted to escape were designated 'N.N.' prisoners, the N.N. standing for Nacht und Nebel (Night and Fog). These prisoners also wore a yellow patch with three black circles over their heart. They could be shot for the slightest misdemeanour and were not allowed any mail or communication with other persons.

The prisoners were divided into 'blocks', each of which had an SS officer in charge of it: 'They were all without exception incredibly brutal ... allowed to hit, kill or torture at will.' Prisoner overseers were appointed to administer and discipline each block. Often these senior prisoners ('Kapos') were even more sadistic than the German guards:

They were usually German and chosen from among the common criminals (e.g. murderers) or sexual perverts (e.g. sadists): for some time the chief prisoner was a sexual pervert from Hamburg. They had full disciplinary authority over the other prisoners in their block and were allowed to beat or strike fellow prisoners. In fact in 1943 when things were at their worst, if a Kapo were to kill another prisoner it would have been completely overlooked.

A story of an incident which happened in 1943 well illustrates the attitude of the Kapos. Some prisoners were working in the quarry and a fall of rock caught and crushed the leg of a Russian prisoner. He took the accident very bravely but was in tremendous pain. The German doctor applied a tourniquet of dirty rags and sawed off the crushed foot. He then poured a bottle of neat iodine on to the raw wound, laughing as the prisoner lost consciousness with pain. The Russian was carried back to his hut where he lay for several days before he died. But during the time he lay there he used to moan and cry with pain as the leg festered. So every so often the Kapo would walk over and thrust the dying man with a heavy stick telling him to shut up.

Galitzine recorded the prisoners' grim daily routine, including eleven hours of work in return for 'a small crust of bread and a bowl of thin "soup" three times a day'. As a result, he wrote:

Many prisoners got swollen or distended stomachs from under-nourishment, all became very weak and succumbed to dysentery, constipation and many other illnesses. The Russians seemed the worst hit and pathetic sights are recounted of Russians eating grass and even dung. Some used to hunt for worms in the mud of a little spring in the quarry. A pathetic description was given to me of a little Lorrainer who died of hunger in the quarry in the summer of 1943. He was left to die and no-one was allowed near him.

Four members of the Luxembourg resistance movement were among the ex-prisoners interrogated by Galitzine. Josef Freismuth, Mathias Barbel, Adam Konrad and Leopold Schilling contributed information on the horrific treatment of prisoners in 'two rooms in the crematorium' from where 'cries and shouts could be heard all over the camp'. They witnessed other barbarous acts: 'executions by hanging and shooting in the neck were carried out almost daily ... 92 women and approximately 300 men were killed during the night of 1st to 2nd September 1944. The corpses were stacked up in a cellar, in which the blood was 20 cm. high.'

Although Struthof-Natzweiler was not an extermination camp (as were such camps as Auschwitz, Treblinka and Sobibor), it included both a gas chamber and a crematorium.

A special gas chamber for experimenting in lethal war gases was built down at the old Struthof hotel in early '43. There was a little glass panel at the side to enable doctors to watch victims' reactions and a hole in the door for the insertion of a gas cartridge.

Each prisoner was fed well a week before being gassed. A special card was kept on the intended victim. Sweets and cakes were given on the day of the experiment. Some even got out alive when the gas failed to work, but they always died in some other way later. The doctors tried to 'revive' patients by injections as antidotes to the gas.

Most of the victims in the gas chamber were women, some 150 were killed in this way including 50 Polish women who were put in at once, one coming out alive. They were stripped first, raped and then crammed into the small chamber (about 12 ft by 12 ft).

In the crematorium there is another room where prisoners were also killed by carbon dioxide gas from the furnace of the crematorium. In here most Jewish victims were killed ...

The crematorium is the most interesting and the most horrible building in the camp. There are flights of steps leading down to a small room where many victims were probably shot as they were forced down the steps. Here in this room the bodies were stacked and fed into a lift which took them up into the furnace room. Here the operator used to put as many as three bodies at a time into the furnace.

Outside lies a pile of coffins used to carry the dead from the dead sandpit or the distant gaschamber.

Possibly the most horrific evidence was the discovery of 120 bodies of prisoners in the Anatomical Institute of the Strasbourg Hospital. Galitzine reported:

Apparently acting on a telephone call from Prof. Jung, head of the Institute, the Camp Comdt sent two lorryloads at 0500 hrs next morning of bodies, naked and still warm when they arrived. They appeared to be 'still alive' having been injected with serum. Some were women. The bodies found were preserved in alcohol in jars, some being already cut up. The prison numbers of all the bodies are available which will permit identification.

It proved difficult for Captain Galitzine to discover much in the way of concrete information about British inmates of the camp. But the rumour he had heard on his first visit was confirmed by one of the witnesses. 'I did in fact find someone who'd been hidden in the village,' Galitzine recalls, 'a prisoner who'd escaped.' But the evidence was thin:

It is reported that there were two Englishmen in the camp – one officer and one professor. The latter left some drawings of his fellow prisoners which he managed to smuggle to one of Stadler's foremen, M. Nicole. These drawings bear the signature – 'B. J. STONEHOUSE'.

The only other information Galitzine could gather on the fate of British prisoners was to prove inaccurate but nevertheless valuable to the Secret Hunters:

One day three women 'spies' were brought up by car to the camp and shot in the sandpit. They were described as being one English-woman and two Frenchwomen, and all were 'well dressed'.

Galitzine was certain that his report sould provoke a storm of rage at SHAEF headquarters in Paris. He expected the massive press corps to be alerted. Instead, it was suppressed. Galitzine could not understand:

I got a rude signal back from headquarters saying that I wasn't to discuss this with anyone else and I couldn't understand. I thought here was something the Allies were going to make something out of. I still to this day cannot understand why the first concentration camp we ran into, why an indication wasn't given to all the armed forces as to what they might expect. The only explanation that was ever given, which was possibly a plausible one, was that it might make the Germans resist all the more and that they would feel that there was no hope. That if everyone was branding the whole of Germany as being responsible for this, the Germans would never give up.

It was difficult enough for Yurka Galitzine to accept official indifference to his report, harder still to understand the reaction of individuals confronted with the facts. Denis Johnston, a war correspondent, visited Natzweiler after the camp was cleared up and was being run by the French as a concentration camp for alleged collaborators. Johnston had some difficulty in gaining admission but 'two packets of cigarettes did the trick'. In *Nine Rivers from Jordan* he describes the camp and the conversation which took place with Galitzine in the evening:

We were shown the alleged torture chamber, gassing room and cremation oven, all of which showed no signs whatever of having been used for such purposes ...
– But it's true, said Yurka that night in Saverne, as we laid out a bed for him on the floor. They are murder camps.
– Oh, come off it, I said. People die in wartime – we all know that. But in the privacy of our room let's try to give things their right names, and keep some sort of perspective.
– If you'll come back with me to Strasbourg in the morning I'll show you the pickled bodies that they left behind – bodies they were experimenting upon.

– I'll do nothing of the sort. Even if you did show them to me it wouldn't prove anything.

– It proves what kind of people we are up against in the Nazis. The trouble with you is, you don't want to have anything proved to you.

– I certainly don't want to have it proved that the human race is different from my own experience of it. Hitler tells us that the Jews are monsters, and I don't believe him. Nor do I believe you when you try to prove that the Germans are monsters. I've met Germans.

– But it's a question of fact. You should never have been shown around that camp by a stupid liar.

– You mean we ought to have had a more subtle guide, eh?

– You should have had somebody who could tell you the facts – the facts that you don't seem to want to face. I wonder why not?

With a deep sense of frustration, Galitzine was assigned to other duties. At the end of the war he was offered the chance to transfer to the War Crimes Investigation Branch at the War Office, which he jumped at:

I said: My goodness me, this is something really that's got to be pursued, because by then we'd heard of Belsen and other things. My own personal experiences made me strongly aware of the whole war crime picture and a feeling that something ought to be done about it. But I had a feeling that even by V-E Day, the impetus was beginning to sort of slacken and people were beginning to say: Well, it's peace, let's forget what's gone before.

This impression was quite correct, as he was to discover when he joined the War Office Adjutant-General's Branch 3 – Violation of the Laws and Usages of War – and moved into an office at 20 Eaton Square in London. It was some months after his experiences at Natzweiler, but he was due to be confronted with the place once again.

5

A mass grave at Gaggenau

In the chaos of defeated Germany, the British authorities felt that there were more important matters to attend to than catching Nazis, let alone accounting for relatively few missing Britons. Literally millions had to be fed, a completely new civil administration had to be forged and the most pressing requirement was for demobilisation. The war was over and those who had fought in it wanted to go home and take up the threads of their civilian lives. The problem was that the occupying forces constantly became confronted with the evidence of atrocities wherever they looked – more than eighty concentration camps, work camps and sub-camps came to light in the British zone alone.

Lieutenant Colonel Gerald Draper, head of the legal department of the War Crimes Investigation Unit, remembers the conditions:

In one word, chaotic. The whole of the population was in movement: refugees fleeing from the eastern provinces of Russia, coming into zones occupied by the British, the Americans and the French in the west; German people returning to towns that had been heavily bombed, and who'd been in the country to avoid the Allied bombing; prisoners of war in their thousands, being returned from POW camps by road transport along the autobahns, in order to get in the harvest. Operation Barleycorn was the primary exercise of the summer of 1945, because the Allied governments feared a famine and a famine means illness . . .

You saw every sign of human distress and misery and if you stopped to eat rations, children appeared out of nowhere and stood in front of you in a row and watched everything you ate, until you threw the food at them and you left . . .

Then there was the physical accommodation in which one had to work. They were just requisitioned houses. My first filing cupboard for war crimes' files was a woman's wardrobe out of which the dresses had to be removed. And I then had to restrain my driver from using some of the better dresses for polishing the car...

Our job was virtually impossible, and at the very early stages we had virtually no investigators. Such as we had, had all been seconded up to Belsen and yet at our desks every day there was a stack of such documentation like a tidal wave.

Lieutenant General Leo Genn's No. 1 War Crimes Team, established in May 1945, was concerned solely with preparing a case against the staff at Belsen. The facts which emerged caused a wave of horror and disgust throughout Britain. Compared with the murder of thousands, the disappearance of British servicemen and women could wait. But this was not good enough for Brian Franks, Commanding Officer of 2 SAS.

At the end of the war the various detachments of the British SAS returned from Germany and Norway to their base at Wivenhoe. The men were either posted back to their parent regiments or returned to civilian life. There was no place in the post-war forces for specialist élite units and by October the SAS had ceased to exist.

Meanwhile, the men who returned from prisoner-of-war camps were interrogated by the SAS intelligence section in an attempt to determine what had happened to those who were unaccounted for. Of particular interest to 2 SAS and to their Commanding Officer Colonel Franks was to find out what had happened to the thirty-one men who had not returned from Operation Loyton in north-eastern France. Major Eric (Bill) Barkworth, who had been their Intelligence Officer during the war, was put in charge of the SAS War Crimes Investigation Team. He was assisted by C.S.M. Fred (Dusty) Rhodes.

One of the first prisoners to return was Sergeant Seymour, the sole surviving captive taken during Operation Loyton, who had broken his ankle on landing. He had been taken to the camp at Schirmeck and from there to the Gestapo head-quarters in Strasbourg. One of the German witnesses stated that 'he was not reluctant to give information', which may well be the reason why he was subsequently transferred to a regular prisoner-of-war camp. He reported that he had seen no other SAS prisoners and that he had not been badly treated. Seymour was of little use to the SAS as a witness.

The first concrete information to arrive at Wivenhoe came from the French and had been passed on via the War Office Casualty authorities. Just to the east of the Rhine, near the famous spa of Baden-Baden, is the small town of Gaggenau in which was situated a large Mercedes-Benz factory. Not far away in the village of Rotenfels there had been a sub-camp of Schirmeck. When Schirmeck had been evacuated towards the end of 1944, many of the prisoners had been moved east of the Rhine. The French occupation authorities, acting on a tip-off, discovered a mass grave at Gaggenau containing twenty-seven bodies, some of which were identified as British and American.

On the strength of this somewhat tenuous lead, Barkworth approached his Commanding Officer, Colonel Franks, for permission to take a small team to Europe in search of information. At the end of May 1945, Barkworth, Rhodes and four others left for the Continent in a jeep and a 15 cwt. Bedford truck – little knowing that their quest would take them two years and over vast distances.

The small convoy drove to Dover where they shipped across the Channel and called in to Paris on the way for Barkworth to make contact with SHAEF headquarters. From there they travelled on to Gaggenau.

The area in which the Barkworth team intended to start their search was in the French zone of Germany, where British troops were seldom seen. It was obvious that supplies, fuel and administrative back-up would be a problem though to begin with the SAS headquarters at Wivenhoe was still functioning and communications were handled by a high-power radio operated by personnel from the 'Phantom' signals brigade.

Finding a missing person in the chaotic conditions of Europe was like looking for the proverbial needle in a haystack. The Barkworth team, however, had certain advantages. Barkworth spoke fluent German and good French and his men were all highly motivated – they were looking for comrades.

On arrival in Gaggenau on 10 June, Barkworth's team

moved into a requisitioned villa that was the property of the Degler family who owned the local brewery. Herr Degler had been imprisoned by the French for being a Nazi, but his wife and two teenage daughters were commandeered by the Barkworth team to do the cooking and cleaning.

The first job was to find out about the bodies which had been discovered in the town some while previously. As Americans were believed to have been involved, also on the spot was a US War Crimes Investigation Team commanded by Colonel Chavez, based at Karlsruhe. Both teams met up at the Waldfriedhof (Forest Cemetery) situated in wooded country on the edge of the town.

What had happened was as follows. On 25 November 1944, the commandant of Rotenfels camp received orders for the execution of all British and American prisoners held there, most of whom had been transferred from Schirmeck. Ten prisoners of war, three French priests and one French civilian were taken into the woods near the cemetery, were shot in groups of three and their bodies tumbled into a bomb crater which was then shovelled full of earth.

Five days later, nine French civilians, all members of the Alliance de Bordeaux, including Monsignor Jean Bordes, were shot and pushed into an adjacent crater. On top of them were dumped four more bodies, all French and including one woman. (She alone has never been identified and still lies buried anonymously in Gaggenau.)

Local witnesses informed the French occupation troops immediately they arrived and the bodies were exhumed. They were said at the time to have been in a good state of preservation but after being left for eight days in the sun, advanced decomposition set in. At that stage another French unit arrived, removed various items from the bodies – unfortunately without determining from which corpse and crater – and reburied all twenty-seven in four rows in the nearby cemetery.

The first priority was to dig them all up again. Colonel Chavez had a highly professional pathologist attached to his team, who set up a temporary mortuary in the Chapel of Rest in the cemetery. The digging was done by the management of the nearby Mercedes-Benz factory. The factory had made use

of prisoners supplied from the Rotenfels camp throughout
the war, and from the state of the prisoners the management
would have been fully aware that they were ill-treated and
starved. Fred Rhodes supervised the digging squad and remembers his feelings at the time: 'We felt that they had been
responsible for the people being shot and killed. We thought
that nobody could shed that responsibility. So many of them
said that they didn't know anything about it. Well, I don't
believe that.'

As the digging progressed, the grisly remains were uncovered, watched by men who had personally known some of the
victims. Fred Rhodes was to become accustomed to decom-
posed bodies during the following two years:

Sometimes there was just a faint resemblance but you must remember, bodies that have been buried for a reasonable time decompose
very quickly.

You could pick out the features of certain people you knew well.
You could say: Yes, this is Captain So-and-So, or this is Lieutenant
So-and-So, or this is Sergeant So-and-So. But you couldn't always
do that, and identification like that wasn't sufficient for the authorities. You had to have firm identification, such as teeth.

Within ten days some positive identifications had been
made on the basis of tags found on bodies – Captain Whately-
Smith, Major Reynolds and two American airmen. In addition, four more of the Loyton prisoners were tentatively
named. Private Griffin, whose body was clothed in army issue
shirt and pants, was identified on the basis of dental charts
and correct height. In addition, a photograph known to be his
had been taken by a Russian prisoner detailed to bury the
bodies and was subsequently handed over to the Swiss Consul
in Baden-Baden. One body was wearing a wrist watch, the
number of which corresponded to the watch issued to Lieutenant Dill. Two further bodies exactly matched the dental
records of Captain Gough (Special Forces) and Private Ashe.

The Barkworth team were extremely busy, working under
immense difficulties. A few more men came over from England to help, and the jeep patrols fanned out in search of
evidence of the other victims as well as the whereabouts of the
perpetrators. The basement of the Villa Degler was turned

into a mini prison and a neighbouring house was commandeered to provide extra living quarters. Within a month of their arrival, Major Barkworth was able to issue an interim report concerning the fate of the missing SAS personnel, as well as details of other crimes against Allied personnel which his team had discovered.

This report is concerned mainly with the Schirmeck camp. The chief personnel are listed, together with photographs and a rundown of Gestapo personnel known to have been active in the area. A considerable number of witnesses had been interviewed, mainly ex-Schirmeck prisoners, and Karl Buck, the camp commandant was under arrest. Roger Souchal had returned alive from imprisonment. He told of horrific beatings meted out to Captains Gouch and Whately-Smith and Lieutenant Dill at the Gestapo base at Saales.

The man they most wanted to catch was Oberwachtmeister Heinrich Neuschwanger, who was alleged to have fired the shots at Gaggenau and was primarily responsible for beatings of prisoners carried out at Schirmeck. Two French priests stated that Major Reynolds was so badly beaten that bones became visible. In August 1945, Neuschwanger was discovered, arrested and taken by Barkworth and Rhodes to the scene of his crimes. Rhodes described what happened, and the only time when he lost his temper with a prisoner:

In particular I remember that we brought Neuschwanger back to the scene of the crime and took him to the bomb crater. Our officer commanding, Major Bill Barkworth, was speaking to him and asked him what were his feelings about the murders that had taken place when the war was practically finished. He just stood there in a very arrogant sort of way but he didn't seem to have any feelings whatsoever.

Barkworth turned and looked at me and I looked at him thinking about the people that we knew personally – that's when my temper went.

So I knocked him to the bottom of the bomb crater, into about eighteen inches of water that was in the bottom. But he was fortunate because he was coming out. The people that had gone in there before weren't. We allowed him to come out and took him back to prison, gave him a bath and that was that.

By the late summer of 1945 Galitzine had become involved closely with the Barkworth team, his office in Eaton Square acting as a clearing house for information and for liaison with the official side of war crimes investigation. When the threat of disbandment brought Colonel Franks to his office, Galitzine was keen to help. It was during lunch, he recalls, that Franks broke the news:

He said, 'I've been told to demobilise the regiment. Is there any means you can keep this team going?'

So I said, 'Well, leave it to us and we'll do what we can.' And in fact, quite without permission at all, merely because after the war there was obviously quite a lot of administrative confusion, one managed to keep the momentum going of pay and rations and everything else...

A signaller was installed in the loft of 20 Eaton Square and the unit in Germany was paid directly by the War Office. Even after the SAS ceased to exist on 8 October 1945, Franks and Galitzine managed to keep in existence the SAS Secret Hunters.

Galitzine visited Gaggenau and was impressed with the efficiency of the small but dedicated team: 'Barkworth was a quite remarkable man, a mystic I would say, a thinker, absolutely dedicated to the job he had of looking for his missing people.'

Fred Rhodes describes him as 'a very eccentric person. He could be arrogant, he could be amusing, he could be the most awkward person that one could ever wish to meet. But at the same time he was a very loyal person, he was very loyal to the people who worked for him.'

But opinions differed about Barkworth. To many of the official war crimes people, he and his men were regarded as a bunch of troublemakers who got results in a highly unorthodox manner. Barkworth's disdain for operating through official channels earned him the open hostility of the British Army. Galitzine recalls the difficulties Barkworth encountered:

You had tremendous co-operation with the French zone and the American zone but in the British zone you had absolute antipathy -

at one stage he was actually forbidden to operate in the British zone, which made life very difficult indeed.

Arthur Harris, the Assistant Adjutant-General for 21 Army Group, was in charge of the British Army zone. Galitzine remembers going to see him:

He actually was well aware of Barkworth's good qualities. But he used to say to me: 'Frankly, there are times when I just cannot help him, because he's his own worst enemy. He will in fact insult generals or brigadiers or he will do things which he knows you're not allowed to do in the army. He'll walk into a mess improperly dressed or he'll bring a sergeant-major into the officers' mess, that sort of thing.

At the beginning of August, General Leo Genn's No. 1 team finished the investigation into Belsen and was drafted into the French zone to help Barkworth. A month later they left.

The problem was that Genn's team did not have the degree of commitment which Barkworth expected. Galitzine witnessed the animosity between the two men. He reported to Arthur Harris:

The team was staffed with inexperienced and unenthusiastic personnel and seemed to have been under a misapprehension as to their task. Lt. Col. Genn stated that the teams' task was 'to put into legal form already existing evidence'. Investigation was not recognised as a job of the team. No attempt was made to find bodies or to dig about for evidence, but they purely went over ground already covered or went after witnesses known to exist. Lt. Col. Genn himself remarked to Major Barkworth and Capt. Scott that 'the *difficulties of organisation are so great, that I am only marking time*'.

Galitzine's report ended:

It must be admitted that the SAS team are all personal friends of the missing men whose cases they are investigating and also of their families, and in addition are inspired by the *esprit de corps* of their regiment. But it is pointed out that if the undesirable spirit of the BARO is left to continue unchecked, only poor results can be expected.

By the end of September Genn had departed. Left to their own devices again, the Barkworth team got on with their dual task – to find the bodies of the missing men and to hunt for those responsible. After the Gaggenau case had been more or less tidied up, the search was concentrated in the Moussey area.

6

The hunt centred on Moussey

In Moussey churchyard ten graves bear the SAS crest. Four are marked 'killed in action': Signalman Bannerman, Lieutenant Castellain, Corporal King and Sergeant Lodge.

On 20 August 1944, the body of Sergeant Lodge had been taken to Moussey for burial by two Frenchmen acting on orders from the Germans. According to the priest, Abbé Gassmann, the body had a wound in the head and bayonet wounds in the stomach. As there was no evidence to suppose that Lodge had been killed after being made a prisoner, it was felt that a war crime could not be proved. Thus Lodge's grave is marked 'killed in action'.

Sergeant Davis became separated from his patrol in the woods on 17 August and three days later he asked the parish priest at Sauley, Abbé Colin, for food, but was refused. The priest then went to the headquarters of *Kommando* Schöner at the Château de Belval, and while he was there a truck left for the village and returned with the soldier. It would seem that Davis was taken from the Château to Schirmeck camp where he was interrogated and was then brought back to the woods above Moussey. In the spring of 1945 a body subsequently identified as Davis was found by the forester Albert Freine. The assumption was that he was taken back to the area in an attempt to force him to reveal the whereabouts of the main camp, and when he refused he was shot.

Three of the Moussey graves are those of Sergeant Fitzpatrick, Private Elliott and Private Conway. They dropped together on the night on 1/2 September 1944. Elliott fractured his thigh on landing and the three men hid in a wood near a farm. The probability is that they were betrayed by a Frenchwoman, Genevieve Demetz, who was working with the Gestapo – she accompanied a squad from *Kommando* Wenger who arrested the three at the farm on 16 September. Three days later they were brought back to the farm, shot, and their bodies burnt in the apiary.

The last two SAS graves at Moussey are those of Privates Brown and Lewis. They were captured, taken to Schirmeck and then brought back to the hamlet of Le Harcholet where they were shot, together with an unknown Resistance fighter.

The cases without bodies were the most difficult to solve. Private Hall was assumed to have been shot between the camps of Schirmeck and Struthof-Natzweiler and the corpse to have been cremated at the latter place. The St Dié case, which accounted for a further eight missing SAS personnel, was pieced together from the testimony of often unreliable witnesses. The Barkworth team established that Lieutenant Black, Corporals Winder and Iveson, Sergeant Terry-Hall and parachutists Dowling, Lloyd, Salter and Crosier were imprisoned at Schirmeck and shot near St Dié towards the end of September 1944.

La Grande Fosse case concerned the murder of a further eight SAS personnel. Fred Rhodes remembers the sequence of events. The rear party commanded by Lieutenant Dill was captured, together with Roger Souchal, by members of a German armoured unit on 7 October. The men were taken to the factory of Monsieur Gerard at Le Harcholet where they were interrogated and then handed over to the Gestapo detachment commanded by Dr Ernst at Saales. There they were joined by Captain Gough, Sergeant Neville, Private Church and Private McGovern. The two officers, Gough and Dill were later murdered at Gaggenau, but the other ranks were taken out and shot on 15 October in an area of woods known as La Grande Fosse.

The first clues came from a prisoner interrogated by the Barkworth unit in Strasbourg prison. After several visits he stated that eight men had been shot but the nearest he could (or wanted to) remember was that it had taken place some eight or ten miles from Moussey. So, in bitterly cold early November weather, Rhodes and three other men set out in a jeep, faced with a seemingly impossible task. They managed to narrow down the possible area to a quarter of a square mile along the road heading east from Saales. This particular road is very narrow as it winds up into the hills, thickly forested on either side, with only rutted paths leading off to either side and still littered with the remains of bunkers and trench systems from the First World War. After several days they had drawn a complete blank but Fred Rhodes was not going to give up:

One day I decided that we would carry out another search and went back out to the area.

Now on proceeding to the lane which was adjacent to the area of land that we intended to continue searching, we moved from place to place in a reasonably organised method until finally I, being an horticulturist in my own profession, decided that a certain area of growth was slightly different to the rest of the surrounding habitat. I decided that I would then go and look what could have possibly been the cause. Well, I did, and on my first attempt at digging I turned up with a chap's toe and knew then that we'd found the eight missing SAS personnel.

The big toe which came out I put into a matchbox and took back to Gaggenau with me, to my officer commanding, and gave it to him, with my compliments because he was concerned that we weren't moving very fast on that one.

On the basis of the toe, a pathologist was sent to the site to carry out preliminary post-mortems together with a labour squad made up from German suspects who were already in custody. They were made to dig up the bodies of their victims, all of whom had been shot in the back of the head from close range. It was discovered that the eight men had been taken to the spot in two closed trucks which then drove off the road into a narrow forest track. Unterscharführer August Geiger was posted as sentry to keep any possible witnesses away, and the men were then taken one by one, made to strip naked and stand on a low bank at the edge of the track – from where they tumbled forward into a shallow grave. The execution squad had been ordered by Dr Ernst and was commanded by Hauptsturmführer Golkel.

That left three further missing SAS personnel to be accounted for. Private Puttick's body was never found, but had probably been burnt. There was some evidence that he had been held by *Kommando* Wenger at Etival but was taken away by someone from Gruppe Kieffer in a car in which were placed a number of cans of petrol. Lieutenant Silly was last seen near the river Meurthe at the end of Loyton by his comrades. Subsequently he was identified as having been at Schirmeck and Etival. He was the only person on the operation who wore glasses. On 6 December 1944, the French discovered a number of badly burnt bodies under the charred remains of the Barodot forest house. The local doctor was called in to identify the remains but as they were so badly burned he was unable to determine the cause of death and it therefore remains unclear whether they were burned alive or shot first.

The final case was that of Private Wertheim, a German Jew who had at one time served in the French Foreign Legion before joining the SAS. He had been captured while taking part in Operation Pistol which had been mounted at the same time as Loyton, and was seen at Niederbuhl camp by Roger Souchal. Some time early in December 1944 he was taken away handcuffed to another prisoner who was an epileptic. The story was that he was to be transferred to Rotenfels, but as he never arrived there it was assumed that he was disposed of on the way.

By the middle of November, the missing men had been largely accounted for and enough evidence had been collected to merit the preparation of a further report, entitled 'Missing Parachutists'. The report, bearing the SAS crest on the cover, is addressed to the Commanding Officer, 2nd Special Air Service Regiment. It is dated 14 November 1945, a month after the disbandment of the regiment, and is signed by Major Barkworth.

The following passage from the Barkworth report on the St Dié case illustrates the method used to build up a case:

		Between
		14.9.1944
CASE 6	ST. DIE	30.9.1944

Lieut. Black and his party of 4 men Cpl. Winder, Pct. Dowling, Pct. Lloyd and Pct. Salter became separated from the main S.A.S. party during the crossing of the Plaine valley on the 10th of September. They were next seen by Mme. Yorg of Les Colins, sheet 36/16. 436868, at whose house they brewed some tea. Towards evening they continued to the house adjoining the scierie La Turbine 445868. Here already 3 further S.A.S. who had been in an action at La Chapelotte 425874 were hiding, these were Sjt. Terry-Hall, Cpl. Iveson and Pct. Crosier. It was probably the first of these two parties which had made use of a French guide named Gaston Mathieu.

On the evidence of George Zahringer, this Frenchman reported the arrival of these parachutists to a member of the German S.D. in Raon l'Etape named Berger, employed by Kieffer. Berger requested assistance from Kdo.zbV.6 under Dr. Ernst, which at that time was in St. Dié, and a detachment was despatched under Hstuf. Albrecht to effect their capture.

After the ensuing action in which Lieut. Black was wounded in the leg, the French owner of the house was shot by Berger, and his wife was also killed in a manner which is not yet fully clear. The eight prisoners were then taken to Raon l'Etape where Kommando Ernst had an Aussenstelle at La Creche, under command of Teufel.

The British prisoners were seen here by M. Georges Noble who was able to recognise Crosier from a photograph shown to him, and also recollects that one of the prisoners was wounded in the leg.

The following morning they were despatched on foot in the direction of Badonviller, but shortly after crossing the bridge over the Plaine river at the end of the Rue Weswal, Laurette Roos was sent by the German guard to fetch M. Gabriel Chapelier and his milk truck to take the party on as the wounded man had to be carried by the others and progress had been necessarily slow. M. Chapelier states that he drove this party to the house in Badonviller occupied at that time by the Aussenstelle of Kommando Pullmer.

The next trace of this group is that they were seen by various witnesses being driven on the way through Allarmont and Vexaincourt towards Schirmeck. Their arrival at the camp is attested by Karl Buck, Joseph Muth, Mlle. Hertenberger, Mlle. Diebolt, Mme. Spielmont, Leon Dennu and many other witnesses, in particular by Dr. Stoll who dressed Lieut. Black's leg, and whom he remembers by name, and by Edouard Maess who helped to carry the stretcher on which Lieut. Black was lying. The gaiter from his wounded leg was kept by Maess. It bears the name Black on the inside, and is included as an exhibit. (Maess had sent it to the F.F.I. in Strasbourg, by whom it has been used in an exhibition of concentration camp relics for electioneering purposes.)

Either the following morning or 24 hours later, this group left

Schirmeck in a closed truck accompanied probably by Ludwig Schlesinger, who at that time was working with the Gestapo in Strasbourg and/or Le Thillot, but who had visited his wife who operated the teleprinter at Schirmeck camp.

Schmidt has as interesting piece of evidence that Gehrum telephoned from the office in which the former was working, shortly before Black's stick left, to say that they would be shot.

Karl Buck, the commandant of the camp, states definitely that he was ordered to send them to Strasbourg.

Dr. Isselhorst B.D.S. states that they were fetched from Schirmeck in order to enable Schneider to interrogate them at Strasbourg, and that acting on subsequent representations made by Schneider, he gave orders for the group to be shot, about a week after their arrival in Strasbourg. Schneider denies all knowledge of this case.

In this connection it is worth mentioning that the testimony of Georg Zahringer of Kommando Ernst discloses the fact that the identity discs of 'the men who were captured at scierie, La Turbine' were hidden by Pilz, a member of Dr. Ernst's Kommando in the St. Dié area.

He states that Pilz told him that he had taken part in the murder of these same eight soldiers at St. Dié. Dr. Ernst is reported to have exhibited extreme anger with his subordinate Albrecht that he had forwarded these prisoners to Schirmeck without keeping them for unit disposal.

Paul Chavanne, Berger's driver was present at the capture of the party. He states that he drove the prisoners to St. Dié. There is however such overwhelming evidence of their presence at Schirmeck that it is hard to reconcile this information, Chavanne states further that he did not see the group again for some days and then that they had been changed into civilian clothes.

He reports that this party of captured parachutists were shot near St. Dié towards the end of September 1944.

The Concierge of Villa des Alouettes, St. Dié, which was maintained as an Aussenstelle of Kommando Ernst after the move of the H.Q. to Saales, states that French Milice members of Kommando Ernst told her of the arrival of a number of English parachutist prisoners who were confined in the hospital. Her son later saw a pile of uniform clothing and equipment similar to that issued to Lieut. Black's party.

Accused and Suspect Accused

Staf.	ISSELHORST Erich
Ostubaf.	SCHNEIDER Wilhelm
Hstuf.	GEHRUM Julius
Krim. Rat	UHRING Robert
Ostubaf.	SUHR
Hscha.	GRIEM
Stubal.	ERNST Hans Dieter
Hstuf.	ALBRECHT
Ostuf.	VEESE Joachim
Oscha.	BRUCKLE
Uscha.	ZAHRINGER Georg
Hscha.	PILZ Josef
?	BERGER Rudolf
Uscha.	MACHATSCHEK
?	VASSEUR
	JANTZEN

and such other members of Kdo. Ernst as may be involved particularly including the French detachment commanded by Bruckle.

Evidence appended

1. Statement by George Zahringer (1)
2. Statement by Georges Noble
3. Statement by Gabriel Chapelier
4. Statement by Jeanne Hertenberger
5. Statement by Josef Muth
6. Statement by Karl Buck
7. Statement by Erich Isselhorst
8. Statement by Wilhelm Schneider
9. Statement by Georg Zahringer (2)
10. Statement by Marcelle Cacheur
11. Statement by Roger Cacheur
12. Statement by Paul Chavanne

Exhibits

A. Photographs of Lieut. Black's stick.
B. Photostats of dental cards of Lieut. Black's stick.

C. Lieut. Black's gaiter.

D. Jojo code pad issued to Lieut. Black and Pct. Dowling's AB. 64 found at 10 Rue d'Alsace, Strasbourg.

Objectively written and carefully set out, Barkworth's report on the missing parachutists is evidence of the painstaking detective work that had been accomplished in four months of intense activity. In his conclusion Barkworth committed his team to making a determined effort to trace and collect all the accused. 'The hunt would be carried out,' he added:

In the confident expectation that the trial of those concerned will be conducted in such a manner that when the popular clamour of this century has been replaced by that of another, the proceedings will be regarded as an example of strict impartial justice and not of revenge.

The fates of the missing men had been established. The Secret Hunters now intensified the search for those who were guilty of the crimes.

7

The search for the guilty

The Barkworth team ranged all over the British, French and American zones in their search for the guilty, combing the prison camps, checking the statements of witnesses. Once they had located a suspect the team set out to arrest him.

Fred Rhodes remembers making one of his first arrests. Like most such operations it took place at midnight. The team had tracked down Max Kester, a member of *Kommando* Wenger, wanted for the murder of SAS men.

Going into the house we found that there were two children sleeping in a bed in the corner. There was a man and woman who were having supper, bowls of soup on the table, and bread. We informed them that we thought that Max Kester was staying with them. They denied this and said 'no he isn't, we haven't seen Max Kester for a long long time.' We searched the house and then, after we came back down into the small living room, we knew that there was another person there, solely because there were two people eating supper, but there were three bowls of soup on the table and the two children were in bed, and in my opinion were pretending to be fast asleep. So therefore, we knew Max Kester was in that building somewhere.

In the corner of this room there was a door, approximately a yard square, which fitted flush with the wall.

Behind the door, Rhodes discovered wooden steps leading to a cellar. He drew his pistol and went down in the pitch dark, reckoning that as soon as he switched on his torch, 'I'd probably get my head blown off'. But everything was quiet:

There wasn't a great lot of junk down there, except that there was a little box here and a box there and a bit of rubbish and so on. But there was a quite oversized linen basket which interested me.

I recall that I just touched it with me foot and it should have moved quite easily. But it didn't. So I immediately kicked it on to its side and out fell Max Kester.

Barkworth had little time for regulations or red tape in his hunt for criminals. He was not above using simple trickery, aided by his mastery of the German language. Galitzine remembers one particular incident:

He heard that one of the key people wanted was in the Russian zone, near Leipzig, and so he impersonated the Gestapo chief, Schneider, on the telephone – the telephone system was still working in those days, through the various zones – and he said to this Gestapo man: 'I'm on to a frightfully good thing on the black market. If you meet me under the clock in Cologne Railway Station on such-and-such a day, at midnight, I'll cut you in on it and we can share the proceeds together.' And this fellow fell for it, the SAS team were waiting in the shadows and they grabbed the prisoner.

The high-handed methods of the Barkworth team sometimes got them into trouble and even resulted in a reprimand for Rhodes. He set off into the American zone one day to arrest a man who was wanted in connection with the Vosges shootings. Arriving at the house, the landlady said that the suspect was working for the US Army in their legal department, but that he would soon be home. Armed with a photograph of the man, Rhodes and his driver waited outside in their jeep until the suspect walked jauntily down the road, whereupon they arrested him and carted him off to prison. Shortly afterwards they discovered that the Americans were looking all over the place for a Warrant Officer Rhodes who had arrested one of their key German personnel. Fred managed to get a few weeks' leave as it was thought advisable for him to disappear until the furore had died down.

But in between the excitement and the success were periods of boredom at the Villa Degler, when they all seemed to be getting nowhere. Prince Galitzine remembers receiving a radio message from Barkworth that all their leads had dried up, so he decided to visit Gaggenau:

I flew out to Frankfurt and he met me and we drove up that night from the airport to the villa at Gaggenau. On the way up, he said: 'You know, we tried planchette last night – you know, the ouija board.' I became very pompous and rather War Office about it all and said: 'You can't mean that you did this. I mean, it's ridiculous.' And he said: 'Well, why not? If people were killed, I mean presumably they want to tell us what happened to them.' I got very sort of stuffy about it.

That evening, with nothing else to do – there was no electricity at the villa and only a limited amount of food and drink – Galitzine joined Barkworth and four other members of his team round the table:

It was really like playing a game of cards. We put out 1-2-3-4-5 and all the letters of the alphabet and the 'yes' and the 'no' and we had an upturned glass in the middle . . . The first questions and answers were all about German names that we knew about and didn't seem to mean very much and then suddenly an English name came up. I seem to remember the name spelled out was F-o-r-d-h-a-m, Flight Sergeant RCAF No. so-and-so. And it came out so positively that we were rather intrigued. And then – 'Killed at Cirey, in the Vosges', and then it came out with 'Lancaster bomber No. so-and-so', and we asked questions and got the names of the crew. It appeared from the interrogation that three of the crew had been killed on impact. Fordham and another person told us through the planchette that they had been marched out to a limewood, just outside this village, made to dig their own graves and shot in the back of the head.

The six men continued all through the night:

We were all absolutely exhausted but we were taking breaks, then coming back to it. You can imagine, we were all in a high state of excitement and fever and so when the thing came to an end, one further question was asked: 'Did you know the names of any of the Germans involved?' I can't remember the name, but I can use Blomberg because in fact it was a name rather like that.

Two wireless messages were sent: one to CROWCASS, the central wanted register in Paris, asking for information on Germans called Blomberg, in a prisoner-of-war camp; a second message to 20 Eaton Square, asking them to check with the RAF missing persons bureau if there was a Lancaster bomber with the same number. And then, Galitzine recalls:

Lieutenant Colonel
Brian Franks,
Commanding Officer
2 SAS *(right),* and
Captain Yurka
Galitzine *(below).* They
kept the SAS War
Crimes Investigation
Team in existence long
after the regiment was
disbanded.

Above: the crematorium at Struthof-Natzweiler. (Photo: the Wiener Library, London)

Below: photographic evidence of the 'horror of the place', taken by Galitzine: 'coffins lying about' and the furnace into which the 'operator used to put as many as three bodies at a time'.

Left: Major E. W. (Bill) Barkworth and *(below)* his team of SAS investigators at the Villa Degler in the German Black Forest town of Gaggenau. The team is at the table around which Galitzine joined them one evening for a planchette session. The young captain was reprimanded for 'conduct unbecoming in an officer and a gentleman' although the séance 'produced' two bodies and a criminal.

Above: the execution of the partisans: a photograph from an undeveloped roll of film which the Barkworth team found on a suspect.

Below: Lieutenant Commander 'Pat O'Leary', arrested in early 1943. At Struthof-Natzweiler he witnessed the fate of the four women SOE agents.

Above left: André Borrel, the first woman to be dropped into occupied France.

Above right: Sonja Olschanesky: recruited in the field, at first she was not identified as one of the four.

Below left: Vera Leigh, arrested in Paris in 1943. (Photo: The Weiner Library, London)

Below right: Diana Rowden, arrested within four months of her arrival in France.

Above: Rudolf Höss, one time commandant of Auschwitz death camp, shortly after his capture. During interrogation, Höss openly admitted responsibility for the deaths of more than two million people.

Below left: Pohl, the most wanted war criminal caught in the British zone, was located by Captain Harry Schweiger *(below right)* of the No 2 Official War Crimes Unit.

Above: Hauptscharführer Peter Straub, sentenced to thirteen years' imprisonment for his part in the deaths of the four women. (Photo: The Weiner Library, London)

Below: Dr Werner Röhde, sentenced to death for the murder of the four women SOE agents. (Photo: The Weiner Library, London)

Abbé Molière, the courageous priest of Moussey who, in
September 1943, offered his life in exchange for his parishioners.
His brave gesture was later marked by the gift of an SAS beret.

We jumped into these SAS jeeps and roared off in a high state of fever to Cirey, which was about eighty miles away, on the other side of the Rhine – in France. When we got there it was early on a winter's morning and the peasants were just in fact leaving their houses to go and till the fields.

Barkworth, who was no respector of persons, started being fairly rough with them because they didn't like us at all but after a bit of bullying and kicking doors open we found a pair of flying boots in somebody's house. We also found the three unmarked graves of the crew in the churchyard, and eventually the peasants pointed out the limewood which was just outside the village where we actually dug up two bodies.

CROWCASS turned up the information that the French were holding a prisoner of the same name as the ouija board had indicated but who was registered as a private in the army. Barkworth went down to the camp and after a lengthy interrogation the man admitted that he had been in the Gestapo. The reason that he did not feature in the lists held by Barkworth was that he had been posted in late and had not been entered by the time the records of the Strasbourg Gestapo ended with the arrival of French troops in November 1944.

As a result of the seance Barkworth had a criminal and two bodies. Captain Galitzine returned to London to see if such evidence was acceptable, only to find himself in trouble.

I took the transcript, which in fact had been taken down question and answer during this planchette session, and I threw it to a rather elderly War Office secretary who was used to taking down interrogation notes. I remember her setting the thing up and looking very prim, and suddenly, when she got to: 'I was killed at Cirey in the Vosges,' she let out a scream and rushed out of the room. The next thing I knew I was had up before the Adjutant-General, flanked by two other generals, and they said: How dare you do anything like this – conduct unbecoming in an officer and a gentleman, you know, dealing with ouija boards.

But I held my ground and I said: But sir, we've got two bodies and a prisoner. So in a typical army remark, they replied: Well, if you *hadn't* got two bodies and a prisoner you'd be court martialled.

Arrested suspects were lodged in the American prison at

Karlsruhe or with the French in Strasbourg for interrogation. The evidence was passed to the legal branch of 21 Army Group at Bad Oeynhausen. The prisoners were then taken to the Villa Degler at Gaggenau where they were well treated, fed and, amazingly, given the free run of the place. Prince Galitzine found that rather surprising:

Barkworth had a strange hold over his prisoners and he seemed to dispense the law almost, in that the ones he thought were perhaps minimally involved he used to give quite a lot of freedom to, and in fact he'd let them off on parole. There was one chap who was actually sent off, I remember, to go for a weekend to see his wife or his mother, knowing that he would eventually be tried at Wuppertal.

I always had a prisoner attached to me as a batman, and I remember a terribly nice man who was either a station master or a postmaster from Bavaria who'd got involved in some shooting of SAS prisoners. He was a quiet little man, a very good batman – he used to shine my shoes and my buttons for me.

Fred Rhodes remembers several occasions on which he escorted a prisoner in a jeep to see his wife – a trust that was repaid in that none of the Germans attempted to escape.

The investigations carried out by the Barkworth team went on into the spring of 1946. In less than a year a vast amount of positive work had been accomplished, the result of which would be tested before a military court. In addition to the SAS murders, they uncovered evidence of the deaths of a number of Allied aircrew, and the horrific end of four British women agents at Stuthof-Natzweiler.

8

Imprisoned SOE agents

Like the SAS, the Special Operations Executive (SOE) was
born to fulfil a need spawned by war and to be the teeth
behind Churchill's promise 'to set Europe ablaze'.* Broadly
speaking, its purpose was not intelligence gathering, which
was left to existing departments, but rather sabotage and
support for resistance movements.

SOE's French affairs were divided into two sections. 'RF'
was British administered but the agents were supplied by de
Gaulle and worked on his behalf. Section 'F', commanded by
Colonel Maurice Buckmaster, was a wholly British enterprise
which ran a considerable number of circuits in co-operation
with French resistance networks.

Acting under Buckmaster was a remarkable woman, Vera
Atkins. One of her responsibilities was to select many of the
women agents sent into occupied France. Women were recruited into SOE to act as couriers and sometimes as radio
operators, rather than to engage in active sabotage. They
were chosen on the basis of being either French born or half
French and with the ability to pass themselves off as native – a
vital attribute for a courier.

One of the earliest women to be sent into France, and the
first by parachute, was Andrée Borrel. Only twenty years of
age and using the cover name of 'Denise', she was dropped
not far from Paris in September 1942 to act as courier for
François Suttill, the head of the Prosper circuit.

By the beginning of 1943 Suttill and Borrel were receiving
regular supply drops, much of which was passed on to communist groups in the Paris area. By the spring the Prosper
organisation had mushroomed, with contacts stretching from
the Loire to the Belgian border. Such an unwieldy circuit was

*An excellent summary of its birth, aims and achievements is *S.O.E.: An
Outline History of the Special Operations Executive 1940-46* by M. R. D.
Foot, BBC, London 1984.

easily penetrated. Shortly after midnight on 23 June, Suttill and Borrel were arrested. Their capture put an end to Prosper and of the horde of circuits associated with it.

Sonya Olschanesky was the fiancée of Jacques Weil, second-in-command of Juggler, a circuit allied to Prosper and also based in the Paris region. When Juggler was penetrated, Weil escaped to Switzerland but Sonya continued working on her own. She was arrested in January 1944. As she had been recruited in the field and had never been sent back to England for training, SOE knew very little about her.

Vera Leigh ('Simone') arrived in May 1943 by Lysander to join the Inventor circuit run by Sydney Jones and based in Paris. She was forty years old, a dress designer by profession and during training had distinguished herself as a crack shot. Bardet, a traitor in the pay of the Abwehr (counter-intelligence) betrayed her and Jones's bodyguard on 30 October and they were arrested at a café in the Place des Ternes.

Diana Rowden ('Pauline') was flown in by Lysander in July 1943 to act as courier for John Starr's Acrobat circuit, based in the Burgundy region. Within four months disaster struck. In November Diana Rowden was arrested in Lons-le-Saunier.

Although given military rank and status as officers, the SOE agents worked in civilian clothes and were covered by forged papers. All agents, both men and women, were well aware of their fate should they be captured in occupied France. They were normally lodged at Fresnes prison and taken for interrogation to the offices of whichever security service had been responsible for catching them.

Brian Stonehouse spent Christmas 1942 in Fresnes. Before the war he had worked as a fashion illustrator and in 1939 had become a gunner with the Honourable Artillery Company, the famous London Territorial regiment. From there he was recruited as a fluent French speaker into SOE and parachuted into France at the age of twenty-one on 1 July 1942. Using the code name 'Celestin', his mission was to act as radio operator for a circuit in the Tours area, but on arrival he was packed off to Lyons and it was not until August that he was able to start transmitting. On 24 October he was picked up by direction finders and was caught at his set. The rest was routine. A progression through a couple of provincial prisons, then imprisonment at Fresnes. Solitary confinement and interrogation followed. Stonehouse kept silent and retained his sanity by reading the torn up sheets of old newspapers which were provided for toilet purposes. On Christmas Eve 1942 he was told that he would be shot as a spy, but for some reason, perhaps bluff, he was allowed to live. Moved on through a succession of camps, Struthof-Natzweiler, Mauthausen and Dachau, in the company of a small group of other British captives, he survived to greet the American liberators of Dachau in April 1945.

Through much of his captivity, Brian was accompanied by 'Pat O'Leary'. Albert Marie Guerisse, to give him his real name, was a doctor in the Belgian army before the war and, refusing to accept his country's surrender, was evacuated from Dunkirk. He made his way back to France and after the final collapse succeeded in reaching Gibraltar. There he was commissioned into the Royal Navy as Lieutenant Commander Patrick O'Leary and joined HMS *Fidelity*, an ancient French merchantman which was used for clandestine operations along the coastline. During one of these forays into Vichy France, O'Leary was captured by the police and imprisoned in Nîmes. Posing as a French Canadian RAF officer, he escaped with the help of Captain Ian Garrow, a Scottish officer who had been left behind in France and had started an escape network for Allied aircrew. When Garrow was arrested, Pat O'Leary took over the organisation and built it into the most successful of its type, returning more than a thousand aircrew to Britain. Eventually however, the Pat Line was penetrated and in early 1943 he was arrested.

More than a hundred of 'F' Section's agents fell into enemy hands, only twenty-six of whom survived the Gestapo prisons and the concentration camps. Two of them, Stonehouse and O'Leary, were the 'professor' and the 'officer' mentioned in Galitzine's report on Struthof-Natzweiler. Three of the survivors were women: Odette Churchill, Yvonne Baseden and Eileen Nearne.

It was Vera Atkins' concern to discover the fates of four of her women which brought her together with the Secret Hunters.

9

The quest of Vera Atkins

As the few surviving SOE agents returned at the end of the war, it rapidly became apparent that many had disappeared without trace. Like the SAS, SOE was due to be disbanded and most of the staff were naturally interested in the future. There was one notable exception: Miss Vera Atkins. She felt a responsibility for 'her people', and determined to find out exactly what had happened to them and to render an account to their families: 'You owe people something, after all, who have fought for you and risked their life for you and with whom you've been directly involved...'

One of the first agents to return was Brian Stonehouse who had been liberated by the Americans from Dachau, together with Pat O'Leary, Bob Shepherd and John Hopper.* All four had been prisoners at Struthof-Natzweiler before being transferred to Mauthausen and finally Dachau. Stonehouse's reappearance tied in with a report concerning Struthof-Natzweiler which Vera had received from a certain Captain Galitzine, whom she did not know at the time.

When camps were liberated and prisoners were discovered claiming to be British agents, there was usually a considerable amount of suspicion at first on the part of the army. But when identity had been established, special military transport was laid on to bring the people home. Vera made a point of personally meeting each and every one of the 'F' Section survivors. She described such homecomings as always dramatic and rewarding.

When Brian Stonehouse and Bob Shepherd arrived back at Northolt, Vera was waiting with a car:

---

*Hopper was not attached to SOE but was a British citizen who had been brought up in France before the war. When the Germans occupied France he set out on a brief but spectacular career in Normandy and Paris as a 'freelance' agent, waging a one-man war against the invaders.

I remember very well exactly what they were wearing. They had decked themselves out rather tastefully in fact, with American boots with trousers tucked into them and loose jackets and I should think about five yards of blue silk material, dotted white, wound around them as scarves, which they had pinched from the Industrihof which was the workshops attached to the camp, and one of these was donated to me. Close-shaven heads, hollow-cheeked, very bright-eyed. Both of them tall, needless to say, slim, Brian very dark brown eyes, long sensitive face. Bob, fair, blue-eyed, round amused robust face. With these two no emotion other than joy. Brian Stonehouse I had reserved a room for in Chelsea Cloisters . . .

Stonehouse told Vera Atkins that in the summer of 1944 he had seen four British women brought to the camp at Natzweiler. She asked him to make a statement on his experiences in the form of an affidavit. In the first part, Stonehouse recorded the incident of the women:

I Brian Julian Warry STONEHOUSE, of 513 Chelsea Cloisters S.W.3 make oath and say as follows:

1. From about the middle of June 1944 I was confined as a prisoner in the German Concentration Camp of STRUTHOF/NATZWEILER, where I remained until the evacuation of the Camp in September 1944.

2. During the month of July but before the attempt on Hitler's life which I remember hearing broadcast on the camp wireless I was working on the outskirts of the prison compound engaged in laying a pipeline with other prisoners just inside the wire on the east side of the camp.

3. My attention was drawn to a group of four women accompanied by two S.S. men, one officer and one N.C.O, whom I believed to be Rapportführer, a man whom we had nicknamed Fernandel owing to his likeness to that French actor.

4. The four women were carrying various parcels and one was carrying, what I remember thinking at the time, was a not very good fur coat. There was one tall girl with very fair hair. I could see that it was not its natural colour as the roots of her hair were dark. She was wearing a black coat, French wooden-soled shoes and was carrying

71

a fur coat on her arm. Another girl had very black oily hair, and wore stockings, aged about 20 to 25 years, was short and was wearing a tweed coat and skirt. A third girl was middle height, rather stocky, with shortish fair hair tied with a multi-coloured ribbon, aged about 28. She was wearing a grey flannel short 'finger tip' length swagger coat with a grey skirt which I remember thinking looked very English. The fourth woman of the party was wearing a brownish tweed coat and skirt. She was more petite than the blonde and grey and older, having shortish brown hair. None of the four women were wearing make-up and all were looking pale and tired.

5. As this was the first time that I had seen women at this camp the occurrence clearly stamped itself in my mind.

6. The whole party moved down the path on which I was working and passed me within a few feet so that I was able to observe them very closely. They went down the full length of the path and turned to the left towards the crematorium building, where they disappeared from my view.

7. Later that evening all the prisoners were confined to their huts before the usual time, and by then rumours were flying round the camp that the four women whom I had seen were English and came from Fresnes, and further that the reason for our confinement was that the women were to be executed that evening.

8. I cannot remember with any certainty the further events of that night.

More than forty years later, Stonehouse remembers vividly that July day: 'We thought: what on earth are these women doing here, because they didn't look starved, they were well dressed – you know, sort of like from the real world.'

Pat O'Leary came closer still to the women. He was in the infirmary barrack and remembers being called to the window as the four women were escorted from the top of the camp, down the central path and into the prison block at the bottom:

All of a sudden the face of one turned towards my window, and to my great surprise I recognised Andrée Borrel, a French girl who had been a member of my unit [the Pat O'Leary escape net]. These girls, always escorted by the SS guards, were taken to the gaol. I had a desire to communicate with Andrée Borrel, but I had understood immediately that it was dangerous and impossible.

During the course of the afternoon and taking a great risk, O'Leary managed to work his way from barrack to barrack until he was in the hut nearest to the prison. From there he was able to call out:

I started shouting in English: 'Hello, are you English girls?' And all of a sudden a face appeared behind the bars of the window of the gaol. And I could see the face of a girl and she said to me: 'Yes, I am English.' And then another question was asked, and I said: 'Well why are you there?' And then the face disappeared.

Much later in the evening, it was dark, the order came again to all prisoners to stay in their blocks at the risk of being shot. Looking out of a window of the infirmary, I could see Dr Röhde, the SS doctor of the camp, marching down the big steps of the central alley between the blocks in the direction of the crematorium.

A few minutes later, maybe ten minutes later, a girl was escorted from the gaol across to the crematorium. And then a signal. The signal of the chimney, which all the prisoners at the camp knew very well. The gust of flame bursting out of the chimney of the crematorium, which meant that the door of the oven of the crematorium had been opened and shut.

Four times a jet of flame shot out of the chimney.

The following morning, one of the guards was seen walking through the camp carrying a fur coat over his arm, presumably the same one noticed by Brian Stonehouse.

Odette Churchill, one of the three surviving women, told Vera Atkins how she had been captured but had escaped death. Her story added a little more to the possible fate of the four women. She had travelled in convoy from Paris to Karlsruhe in Germany with seven other women, all of whom had been agents in the field. They remained in Karlsruhe but she was soon transferred to the women's concentration camp at Ravensbrück. There she was kept in solitary confinement until almost the end of the war when the Russians were about to overrun the camp. The commandant, Fritz Suhren, was convinced she was related to the Prime Minister. He took her in a car and made for the American lines. He obviously

73

intended to use her as a bargaining counter, which did not do him much good – Odette promptly denounced him to the Americans and he was arrested.

On the basis of the information she had collected from Stonehouse, O'Leary and Odette Churchill, Vera Atkins asked Major-General Gubbins, the head of SOE, for permission to go to Europe to investigate. She was told that as the service was closing down, she should forget it. Undeterred, she pursued her quest and went to see Prince Galitzine at 20 Eaton Square. He was somewhat surprised at her visit:

I was sitting in my office and somebody came in and said: 'There's a Miss Atkins to see you.' And she came in and said, 'I believe that you went into Natzweiler when you were in the army in eastern France,' and I said 'Yes'. And she said: 'Did you ever hear anything about any of these women,' and she produced a list with photographs of eight or ten women. And I said: 'No, but I do remember in the report I wrote somebody had told me that two British women had been killed there.'

Both were convinced that the case ought to be followed up, and as Galitzine's position gave him considerable latitude, he was able to get them seats on an aircraft to Strasbourg. From there Vera travelled on to Karlsruhe where she discovered a woman who had been the chief wardress at the prison and who had kept most of the relevant records. 'I interrogated the woman in charge of the prison, which led me to German women who'd been imprisoned, and who confirmed that four women left in one convoy.'

Vera's next problem was to get herself over to Europe on a more permanent basis and with a rank to confer some status in the military environment. By pulling strings with senior RAF connections, she was commissioned as a temporary squadron officer in the WAAF. Galitzine was also active on her behalf, and the War Office grudgingly gave her three months' attachment to Colonel Draper's legal section of the War Crimes Investigation Unit stationed at Bad Oeyenhausen.

Vera made a great impression on all who met her, among them Draper:

Vera Atkins was a very remarkable woman. I don't think I've met anybody like her, or am likely to do so again. She arrived as a very composed, very self-contained, self-assured person with a sense that she conveyed immense reserves of mental ability and purpose. A quiet-spoken woman, who managed to convey to those she addressed the sense of purpose – she was there to do something and nothing, but nothing, was going to deter her...

She was immensely useful to us. She was a very calming influence, and she was a woman whom it was almost impossible to ruffle. She would discuss appalling things that had happened to these women agents, and terrible things did happen to them when they were caught, normally with a degree of detachment, almost a concentration on the technical details of how it had happened and how the mission had led to their capture.

She was a very quiet person, but seemed to do a lot more listening than talking. I thought she was a charming lady, and a very efficient one.

Vera Atkins' first priority was the Struthof-Natzweiler case. The Barkworth team had already done a lot of the basic work. In pursuit of SAS victims they had investigated the camp and had added to the names of camp staff listed in Galitzine's report of December 1944. In addition to Stonehouse, O'Leary, Shepherd and Hopper, they knew of six British inmates: Lieutenant T. Groome, Lance Corporal Frederick Jones, Father Albert Durand, a priest from Jersey, and the Paynters, father and son, from Guernsey. Most of these men had left for Dachau when Natzweiler was evacuated on 4 September 1944.

It seemed probable, too, that Private Hall had died at Natzweiler. Stonehouse described being taken by a Luxembourg prisoner to a room in the camp in August 1944. There he was shown the naked body of a young man. The Luxembourger said that he thought the body was that of an English Commando and that he had been shot. Stonehouse was able to describe the young man as 'short, strongly built with a typical young English face, fresh complexion, fair hair, blue eyes and a small nose', but when shown a photograph of Private Hall he could not make a positive identification.

The Barkworth unit knew that a certain Peter Straub, a

Hauptscharführer in the SS, had been in charge of the crematorium at Struthof-Natzweiler and also acted as the camp executioner. The accounts of his arrest and interrogation differ slightly. Fred Rhodes remembers being sent to Mannheim to a flat where Straub was living. Rhodes was struck by a series of livid scars on Straub's cheek which appeared to have been caused by long fingernails. When taxed with the fate of the women agents, Straub at first stated that he had been on leave at the time of their death and anyway blamed it all on Röhde, the camp physician who was an SS officer.

When Vera, with Gerald Draper, interrogated Straub, he proved more forthcoming and told them quite openly what had happened, taking refuge in the fact that as a minion he was only obeying orders. Draper recalls the meeting with Straub – 'interrogating an extremely unattractive member of the SS concentration camp staff of Natzweiler' – as follows:

There were four women agents, who were alleged to have suffered disposal by the furnace, and the issue was whether or not they had been injected before they were thrown in the furnace or at all. It had been a particular concern, I recall, to Vera Atkins, to ascertain exactly what happened.

It was part of her what I might call dedication to the technical accuracy of her job – apart from the human side of it. And this individual in front of us was the person we had reason to believe had disposed of them into the furnace.

We proceeded to talk about the method of disposing of these agents, and then we moved over to talk about the other executions that he'd carried out, by hanging. We discussed the height of the stool on which the wretched victims stood before it was kicked away. And he was not sufficiently intelligent, this man, to realise the drift of my question until he realised that I was establishing that he had let them die by slow strangulation as opposed to a prolonged drop to break the neck.

At the end of this interview, he referred to the number of 'pieces' he had disposed of in a day, and with that I said: 'You leave this room on your hands and knees like an animal, you are not fit to stand and talk to human beings on your legs.' And that stage, I seem to recall, was the first and only and last time I ever saw Vera Atkins show the slightest form of distress. Normally she sat perfectly

composed, following and indeed suggesting questions and sometimes asking them because she was a skilled interrogator.

Subsequent interrogation of the camp commandant, Hartjenstein, confirmed the sequence of events. He told Vera
Atkins that orders had been received from Berlin for the
execution of four female prisoners classified as N.N., night
and fog, which meant that they were to be destroyed without
trace. Hartjenstein and the other senior officers at the camp
were no strangers to gratuitous cruelty but were not pleased
at having to carry out this task. They discussed between
themselves various methods of destroying the women and
Röhde finally agreed to give each girl a supposedly lethal
injection.

Subsequent interrogation of the camp commandant, Hartjenstein, confirmed the sequence of events. He told Vera
Atkins that orders had been received from Berlin for the
execution of four female prisoners classified as N.N., night
and fog, which meant that they were to be destroyed without
trace. Hartjenstein and the other senior officers at the camp
were no strangers to gratuitous cruelty but were not pleased
at having to carry out this task. They discussed between
themselves various methods of destroying the women and
Röhde finally agreed to give each girl a supposedly lethal
injection.

On the evening of their arrival, the women were taken one
by one from the prison block into the crematorium hut. There
Röhde, on the pretext of giving them a typhus injection,
actually injected phenol which produced fairly rapid but
hardly pleasant death. Each body was then taken along the
corridor and immediately burned by Straub. Although it
could never be conclusively proved, it was probable that at
least one of the victims was still alive after the injection and
that it was she who had scratched Straub's face.

From the descriptions given by Stonehouse, Vera had to
deduce the identity of the victims, which was not easy.
Andrée Borrel's had been confirmed by Pat O'Leary, and the
woman with a ribbon in her hair proved to be Diana Rowden.
Vera Leigh was the petite one with shortish brown hair. The
fourth was incorrectly named by Vera Atkins as Noor Inayat

Khan. At the time Vera was unaware that Miss Inayat Khan had been shot at Dachau. In fact, the fourth Natzweiler girl was Sonya Olschanesky who had never been to England, having been recruited in the field.

Having satisfied herself that the Natzweiler case was sufficiently prepared to go for trial, Vera Atkins turned her attention to the search for witnesses throughout the liberated territories. She became involved in the investigations into the Ravensbrück women's camp where three further SOE agents had been killed. She also helped to track down those responsible for the deaths of a number of male agents in such camps as Flossenburg.

Most of the captured SOE agents had passed through the interrogation centre at Paris Gestapo headquarters, 84 Avenue Foch. Vera Atkins found out that the Paris Gestapo centre's chief, Kieffer, was being held by the French. Bill Barkworth 'borrowed' this key witness and Vera remembers their meeting in the dining room at the Villa Degler:

I had the opportunity of a prolonged and quiet conversation with Kieffer and he started by informing me that of course he always had the greatest concern for our people, for whom he had the greatest admiration, and in particular some of the women and some of the men, whose names he mentioned to me. And he felt that he had a very clear conscience in that they must all have survived. So I quietly told him what exactly he had done, about sending them on with their records, and selecting Karlsruhe for the women for his own convenience, since he happened to live there – it was nice for him to have an excuse to return from Paris whenever he felt like it – and when I told him the fate of one or two he pretended to cry. And I think that I have rarely felt as angry or disgusted as I did at the sight of this man who produced tears.

And I remember saying to him: 'Kieffer, if one of us is going to cry, it's going to be me, and you will please stop this comedy.' Tears really did prove too much for me by way of hypocrisy.

Vera Atkins' meeting with Rudolf Höss, the commandant of Auschwitz, made a lasting impression on her. He had been discovered near Flensburg in North Germany. Disguised as a farm labourer, he had been arrested on the pretext of having stolen a bicycle. She remembers what happened:

One morning I came into the office, rather late as usual, and Group Captain Summerhough said to me: 'You've kept us all waiting.' I was rather surprised, and he said: 'Well, we thought it'd be nice for you to interview Rudolf Höss with Gerald Draper and act as his interpreter.' I said: 'Delighted.' ...

So I went off with Gerald to a little gaol in Minden, which was a sort of private holding gaol where people were kept for the time that they were being interrogated in connection with war crimes, by the legal section.

And there was this little room, which had a window on to a small interior courtyard and they brought in Rudolf Höss, who was in a normal sort of suit, had great white moustaches, and he was very relaxed. Gerald started off by saying: 'Your name is so-and-so?' – in other words, his false name – and he said: 'Yes.' 'And you lived at this farm?' 'Yes.' 'And you did an absolutely dastardly thing, you stole a bicycle from a poor Polish foreign worker?' And he said: 'No, I never did such a thing. Oh no, that's a mistake. That was nothing to do with me.'

Gerald then said: 'We think that you're Rudolf Höss, ex camp commandant of Auschwitz.' Well, this knocked him back a little, and he denied this. So we said: 'Well, all right, think about it,' and pressed the bell for a sergeant to come in. Gerald said: 'Remove this gentleman's moustaches.' And he was taken into the courtyard – and I'll never forget this, because it was such an incredible scene. We all knew who he was, and the sergeant held him gently by the nose, and removed his moustaches and brought him back.

You know you often hear of people's knees knocking, but it is the only time when in actual fact I've seen a man with knees knocking. That was the great Rudolf Höss.

And he very quickly admitted it, because we had photographs of him and everything that was necessary for proof to prove. And so he spoke very freely really of his tenure there. We weren't going into great details, but we were concerned with the number of people gassed during his period, and as usual you prepare yourself for this kind of thing by trying to keep a record of the convoys who went there, and so forth. We reckoned that it probably was in the region of about one and a half million people and we put it to him and he said: 'Oh no, 2,345,000' or whatever it was – corrected it upwards to an alarming degree. And I remember at this point Gerald looking at him and saying: 'There's no reason really to boast, you have no cause to boast. In any case, you are by far and away the greatest murderer, including Nero of antique fame. So why do you say this number?'

He replied: 'Because when I took over the number was so-and-so, and when I left the number was so-and-so. So I know.' And Gerald said: 'Well, are you prepared for this statement to be taken down?' And he said: 'Yes,' and we wrote it down and he signed it. And all this between breakfast and lunch.

Höss was handed over by the British to the Americans who used him as a witness at Nuremberg and from there he was sent to the Poles for trial. He was condemned to death and while in prison he wrote his memoirs, *Commandant of Auschwitz*, a factual and even objective account of his career, written in the form of a report by a successful factory manager. Then he was taken to Auschwitz and hanged in front of what had once been his office.

With her fact-finding task accomplished, Vera Atkins left Germany as quietly as she had arrived, not wishing any form of praise or official recognition.

10

The capture of Oswald Pohl

In September 1945 a second official War Crimes Investigation Unit was formed, specifically to investigate the Neuengamme concentration camp, near Hamburg, and to clear up the backlog of cases arising from the murder of British airmen. But the task it was set was impossible. The unit lacked resources – personnel, typewriters, transport and even furniture. Most of the British investigators had no police training and did not speak German. There were far too few of them.

By the beginning of 1946, only twenty-one cases involving some ninety defendants had been tried, while 241 cases involving British and Allied nationals were awaiting trial; 306 more cases involving British alone were held up because the alleged criminals could not be found. The total of known crimes had risen to 3,678 and the War Crimes Unit had 1,281 prisoners in custody.*

Lieutenant Colonel Alan Nightingale, head of the investigation branch, admits that many of the investigators were highly unsuitable and some were unable to resist the temptations offered in post-war Germany. The very nature of their work led them into the half-world of the black marketeers, smugglers and pimps. Others felt that they had done their bit during the war and simply wanted to enjoy the fruits of victory – which is understandable.

In an effort to solve the chronic personnel problems a number of SAS officers were sent to Germany as investigators. They were joined by a group known as 12 Force, all of whom had served in the German and Austrian sections of SOE during the war. Most of them were of Jewish origin, young, fit and with a strong motivation to join in the hunt for war criminals.

*The whole sorry tale of incompetence and lack of will is set out in Tom Bower's book, *Blind Eye to Murder*, Deutsch, London, 1981 and Granada, 1983.

The task of tracking down wanted men was largely a matter of painstaking detective work combined with a certain element of luck. Evidence was collected of crimes, witnesses were interrogated and a pattern of names would emerge, varying from minor local police officials who might have connived in the murder of a shot-down airman, to the senior SS officers responsible for mass killings in the concentration camps. The investigators worked closely in the British zone with the counter-intelligence authorities and the field security police, both of which frequently had to make use of ex-members of the Gestapo.*

The major cases involved months of work sifting through piles of evidence in the form of statements and captured documents, in an effort to present a watertight case that would stand up in court and with a reasonable chance of producing convictions.

Far and away the biggest fish to be caught in the British zone was SS Obergruppenführer Oswald Pohl who had been born in 1892 in Duisburg. Before entering the SS he had served in the German navy as a paymaster. He joined the Nazi party in 1926. During a visit by Hitler to Kiel in 1933, Pohl met Himmler whom he must have impressed as he was asked to build up the SS administration. Pohl rose rapidly as the SS expanded and at the end of the war he was responsible for the WVHA, a vast bureaucracy dealing with the concentration camps and the SS industrial enterprises, answerable only to Himmler himself. Amt D was the sub-section which directly administered the camps and the extermination policies. Some of its members were arrested in Flensburg and from them it was learnt that the remaining officials of the WVHA, headed by Pohl, had left Berlin for Dachau on 15 April 1945.

Captain Harry Schweiger and Captain Murdoch of 12 Force were given the task of locating Pohl and spent two months building up a picture of his last known movements and those of his associates, travelling 5,000 miles in the process. The first breakthrough came when they located a certain

*Klaus Barbie was employed by the British before he moved south and joined the Americans as an undercover police agent.

Witt living in Hamburg, who had been one of Pohl's adjutants. Witt confessed that he and Pohl had trekked north from Bavaria in May and June 1945, pushing their possessions in a handcart and working on farms in exchange for food. They arrived in Hamburg under assumed names and Pohl had grown a moustache. Witt mentioned that he was later visited by Pohl who showed him a passport photograph of himself with which he intended to obtain a new identity card and said that he was living near Hamburg. He also stated that he had received a postcard from Pohl, which was discovered at the home of Witt's father – it was postmarked Verden, a small town to the south of Bremen.

Schweiger discovered that one of Pohl's sons-in-law, Werner Westphal, was living in Verden with a Mrs Topp – directly opposite the barracks used by the Black Watch Regiment. An observation post was set up on the roof of the barracks to keep the Topp house under observation, while Schweiger visited the local photographers. At one of them he found a set of plates showing a moustached face and on the back was written Ludwig Gniss – which was the name of the father of an illegitimate child born to Pohl's second wife. After following a series of false leads, 'Ludwig Gniss' was finally tracked down to the tiny village of Armsen where he was registered as a gardener working for one of the local farmers. Schweiger's main concern was to carry out an arrest without permitting Pohl to use a cyanide capsule which so many of the senior Nazis carried with them. He set out for Armsen in uniform, accompanied by a German policeman and a corporal in the Black Watch disguised as a Polish displaced person. On arrival, the policeman was sent into the village to ascertain that Pohl/Gniss was there, and discovered him working in a garden. Schweiger then hid and the young corporal, who spoke broken German, went forward with the policeman and accused Pohl of having stolen his bicycle. Feigning anger, the corporal leapt at the unsuspecting Pohl and dived into his pockets – where two poison capsules were discovered.

The German policeman then arrested Pohl and he was taken to the civilian prison in Verden for a few hours while arrangements were made to transfer him to 'Tomato', the small prison in Minden used as an interrogation centre by the

War Crimes Investigation Unit. There Pohl confessed his identity. He was later transferred to American custody to be tried and was hanged at Landsberg prison, one of the last war criminals to be executed.

11

The scales of Justice

War crimes trials in Germany were held by court martial and authorised by a Royal Warrant which had had to be amended to cover cases of crimes committed by Germans against Germans and other non-British or Allied nationals. In addition to punishing the guilty, one of the avowed aims of the trials was to demonstrate the virtues of impartial justice to the German people. A month before the long drawn out process began of trying the major Nazi offenders at Nuremberg, the first of the major set-piece trials was held in the British zone, where the commandant and staff of Belsen faced their judges in Luneburg on 17 September.

Those arraigned consisted of Joseph Kramer, the commandant, and forty-four of his staff including the infamous Irma Grese. Both she and Kramer had previously served at Auschwitz. None of those in the dock was accused of murder, in spite of the 25,000 corpses, only of having been party to the ill treatment of prisoners, thus causing their deaths.

Each of the accused was defended by a serving military officer, who represented their 'clients' as innocent victims of a system that had broken down. The smart, clean prisoners in the dock made a favourable impression while the half-starved ex-prisoners called as witnesses were criticised for being vague as to dates and often as to the exact names of victims.

The result was a scandal that caused an international outcry. Eleven of the accused were sentenced to death, one to life imprisonment, eighteen to imprisonment from between one and fifteen years, and the rest were acquitted. Those under sentence of death were held at Hameln prison. There, Gerald Draper had a last encounter with the commandant at Belsen:

I spent most of the day with him in the death cells, up at Hameln, about a week before he was hanged. Kramer was not a stupid brute

85

of a man; he was highly intelligent, very quick and had, as it were, a thorough grounding in his job. And he expressed to me articulately over a day, keeping two shorthand writers pretty busy, all the people above him whom he thought should be brought to book as war criminals, and he was even indignant that we hadn't yet arrested them, because they were the people who'd given him the orders. His memorable words were: 'I used to say to my wife in the evening at Belsen, after one of these days, I wouldn't like to be the people in Berlin who give me these terrible orders to carry out.'

After the Belsen trial the pace of the courts increased as other cases were made ready for trial before the military justices. During the spring and summer of 1946 a court was convened at Wuppertal to try those responsible for the crimes committed in the Vosges. The courtroom was in the administrative building of the local zoo, in a room that had been used before the war as a banqueting hall. Major Barkworth, Fred Rhodes and others of the SAS team were quartered in the same building, while the defendants were lodged in the civilian prison. The trials lasted through into the summer, with Major Alistair Hunt acting as prosecutor.

One of the first trials concerned the murder of Sergeant Habgood, an RAF bomb-aimer whose aircraft was shot down near Niederhaslach in Alsace at the end of July 1944. Habgood was captured and lodged in the cells at Schirmeck, from where he was collected in a truck by Peter Straub from Natzweiler. No trace of his body was discovered. In the dock were Straub, Hartjenstein, the commandant at Natzweiler, Giegling, who drove the truck, and a certain Berg, a prisoner who acted as Straub's assistant in the Natzweiler crematorium.

What emerged and was proved to the satisfaction of the court was that Habgood was taken to the crematorium and hanged by Straub and Berg while Giegling looked on and smoked a cigarette. A short drop of only a few inches was used and the victim, according to medical evidence, would have taken ten minutes to die by strangulation. The commandant denied all knowledge of the execution, but the prosecution argued that it could hardly be possible for Straub to act as hangman simply whenever he felt like it. Straub, Giegling,

Hartjenstein and Berg were all sentenced to death, and Muth, in charge of the cells at Schirmeck, was given seven years' imprisonment. Muth died later in French custody. Straub and Berg were hanged on 11 October 1946. Giegling and Harjenstein were handed over to the French to answer for other crimes: Giezling was sentenced to ten years and Hartjenstein to life imprisonment.

The Gaggenau case was tried in May 1946 with eleven accused in the dock, a mixture of those who had pulled the trigger and those who had set up the execution. The prosecution had to establish that those who had set up the execution had known of the likely fate of the victims. Five death sentences were handed down, although only one was finally executed by the British. Buck, the commandant of Schirmeck, Nussberger, the security officer, Ullrich and Ostertag were all passed on to the French to be arraigned for the murder of French civilians. Ullrich was shot in August 1947 and the others were imprisoned. Neuschwanger, however, who had personally shot the SAS victims, was reserved for British justice, much to the satisfaction of the Barkworth team. During his trial he had accused Fred Rhodes of ill treatment, that morning by the lip of the bomb crater. Fred was asked by the president of the court if that was true. He produced a leave pass from his pocket showing that he had been in England at the time – a justifiable case of bending the rules.

At five o'clock on the morning of 26 September 1946, Bill Barkworth and Fred Rhodes were admitted to Hameln prison to witness the execution of Neuschwanger. Rhodes was asked if they went there in a spirit of vengeance:

Revenge didn't come into it as far as we were concerned. Revenge wasn't anything that we considered. We had a job to do, and that was to bring these people to justice and once we'd achieved that, then we thought we'd done our work. But revenge, no. We didn't seek revenge.

Barkworth and Rhodes were taken along the prison corridors to the small room where the executions were carried out and took their places among the various officials involved:

He was marched to the place where he was going to be hanged and it was Pierrepoint, the hangman, that was on duty. He came out and did the work that he should be doing and then it was all over. There wasn't a great lot that you could say about it, or even think about it. It was more or less over and done with...

Right up to the moment that he was hung I don't think it worried him one little bit. I don't think he had any sorrow or remorse at all in him, that man, he was cruel.

Barkworth and Rhodes were silent as they returned to their jeep and back to their duties:

It was something that one doesn't want to do more than once. I think it was when we came out of that prison, we were both pleased that we'd come out. Because I believe we were both of the opinion that it's not nice to see somebody die.

The St Dié case dealt with the murders of various of the Loyton victims and lasted from 22 to 25 May 1946. In the dock were eleven members of Kommando Ernst, all of whom had been either involved in or on the fringes of the executions. The prosecution was faced with the problem of accepting evidence from accomplices as there were no impartial outside witnesses to the killings – each defendant told a different story, trying to exonerate himself and to blacken the others. The defence claimed that the victims had lost their prisoner-of-war status by associating with the Maquis and thus could be disposed of as partisans. When that was not accepted by the court, the defence went on to claim that the soldiers were 'judicially executed'. In his summing up, however, the Judge Advocate General made the point that for a judicial execution to be lawful a warrant must be signed by a sovereign authority after a legal and properly constituted trial had taken place. A further piece of casuistry was the claim that as parachutists had not existed at the time of the Hague Convention of 1907, it did not apply to SAS troops.

Predictably the court was not impressed and sentenced the main participants – Griem, Wetzel and Jantzen – to death. Others received prison terms varying from thirteen to three years.

In the case of La Grande Fosse, several of the same defendants had to answer for their activities. This was held the week before the St Dié trial and there was considerable discussion of the 'superior orders' plea, the problem often turning on what was an illegitimate order. As in other trials of men who had killed parachutists, the defence sought protection behind the umbrella of the Commando Order issued by Hitler. In his summing up, the Judge Advocate General said: 'The fact that a rule of warfare has been violated does not deprive the act in question of its character as a war crime, neither does it in principle confer upon the perpetrator immunity from punishment.'

Nevertheless, the court was surprisingly lenient: the maximum sentence awarded was only ten years – for Golckel who had organised and personally commanded the execution squad of eight SAS men at La Grande Fosse. The minor figures were all acquitted and the rest received terms of imprisonment ranging from two to eight years.

Predictably there was an outcry in the press, which at that early date was still very much in the mood for retribution. Also highly critical was the president of the court, Brigadier Hennessey, who protested to the War Office about the unsuitability of the officers who had sat with him.

La Grande Fosse was followed by the trial of those involved in the killing of the four SOE women at Natzweiler. Accused were ten members of the camp staff, including Straub and Berg, already under sentence of death, Hartjenstein, the commandant, likewise condemned, and the camp doctor, Röhde. From the start the defence sought to establish that the women were spies, whereas the prosecution regarded them as communications assistants and thus a legitimate arm of the forces. There was some justification in this, in that women agents were employed basically as couriers and wireless operators not as intelligence gatherers. The fact remained, though, that they had been operating in civilian clothing and under aliases. Several of the defendants claimed that they were of the opinion that there must have been a trial carried out before the women were sent to the camps, otherwise their execution would not have been ordered. This the prosecution was able to refute.

The first witness to be called was Squadron Officer Vera Atkins, who gave the facts as she had been able to discover them, including by now the correct identity of the fourth woman as Sonya Olschanesky, not Noor Inayat Khan. The press and other persons present in the court were given strict instructions that the name, rank and wartime occupation of Vera Atkins were not to be mentioned outside the court-room. Her evidence was followed by the prosecution building up its case on the basis of the contradictory statements made by the accused. What substance was injected into the women, and how much, was never established, nor whether or not they were still alive when they were placed in the furnace. What was beyond dispute was that injections had been admi-nistered by Röhde with the intention of causing death. An important but unreliable witness was Berg, Straub's prisoner assistant. He stated that on the night in question he had been ordered to stay in his room in the crematorium building, after he had lit the furnace. Berg went on to state that he had been able to overhear what went on and he claimed that at least one of the women was still alive and caused the scratches on Straub's face. Apparently he heard one of them ask in French, 'Pourquoi?' (why) and Röhde replied, 'Pour typhus.' Straub maintained in his evidence that Berg had helped him strip the women before burning them.

The court clearly felt that Röhde was the guilty one and sentenced him to death. Straub was given the benefit of the doubt as far as murder was concerned, although the thirteen years' sentence did not alter his previous status in the con-demned cells. Berg was given four years and the commandant life imprisonment.

The Vosges trial required those responsible at the top, the men who had issued the order for *Waldfest* which had led to the deaths of the SAS men, to answer for their deeds. Gehrum, Schneider, Dr Isselhorst, Oberg and Schlierbach were in the dock. They were joined by Lieutenant General Seeger who had been in command of the infantry division ordered to suppress the Resistance in the Vosges. The pro-secution pointed out that he knew about the deaths of the parachutists and took some steps to have them brought be-fore a proper court – which he, as the superior officer, could have convened. Oberg, as the senior ranking police and SS officer in France during the summer of 1944, was held ultimately responsible for the issuing of orders to shoot all captured parachutists within forty-eight hours. In addition he had been the driving force behind the deportation of the French Jews.

Gehrum was acquitted as the court could not find that he was directly involved and much of the evidence against him was doubtful, a fact which must have disappointed Major Barkworth. Schneider was given the death sentence and was executed at Hameln in January 1947. He was the real instigator of *Waldfest* although he naturally claimed that he had only followed orders handed down from above. Isselhorst received the same sentence and was then passed on to the French who shot him for the murder of Resistance personnel. Surprisingly, Oberg, who was also later tried by the French, received only life imprisonment. General Seeger got away with three years.

In a relatively short period of time, with limited resources and official good-will lacking, the British courts dealt with 1,085 war criminals, of whom 240 were sentenced to death.

The Barkworth team and Vera Atkins had accomplished their task: they had delivered those responsible for the deaths of their people into the hands of justice. Vera felt some satisfaction, not with the punishments awarded but that the relatives of the missing personnel would finally know what had happened to them. Bill Barkworth, too, had carried out the orders given to him by Colonel Franks on 15 May 1945. All those missing had been accounted for and those whose bodies had survived had received honourable burial. The regimental records could be put straight.

12

Death cannot be revenged

As the trials came to an end, the Secret Hunters departed with mixed feelings. They took up the challenges of civilian life or returned to regimental soldiering – some even drifted into the nebulous world of intelligence. Those of the hunted who had been imprisoned were all released by the early 1950s and those still at large were able to breathe more easily as they participated in the 'economic wonder' of Adenauer's reborn Germany. Any still alive are now old men who have probably been able to wash their consciences clean. Apart from a few dedicated prosecutors, there is no desire in Germany today to rake over the Nazi past.

If officialdom had had its way, the men who died in the ditch at La Grande Fosse and the four women who perished so ignobly in the crematorium at Natzweiler would have remained 'missing in action'. A few of the more obvious Nazis would have been prosecuted while the rest would have been sent home. It was more important, as far as the occupation forces were concerned, to bring in the harvest and get the German economy back on its feet than to chase war criminals. Today it is easy to feel a sense of righteous indignation that it was necessary for the SAS to mount their own investigation into the fate of their murdered comrades and for Vera Atkins to have had to operate on her own.

All those involved as hunters or prosecutors were in some way affected by their work. People cannot be exposed to such inhuman degradation without it leaving some sort of scar, and yet there was no sense of seeking revenge. All of those spoken to in the course of research made the point that a death cannot be revenged with another death, but that justice was the aim.

At the liberation of Dachau, Brian Stonehouse witnessed the killing of several of the guards and prisoner overseers by the enraged inmates. He and Bob Shepherd personally sheltered a guard to protect him from the mob, not to save his life

92

but to preserve him for eventual trial. Later, Stonehouse went back to Germany as an interrogator attached to the Americans, working in the internment camp at Darmstadt which was reserved for the 'immediate arrest' category – SS, Gestapo, etc. In the summer of 1946 he was offered the opportunity of revenge:

My job was to interrogate a certain number of prisoners every day, make some notes, and the following morning the notes would come back typewritten for me to sign the papers. I always remember, there was this older prisoner who came in, handed me my papers and stood there, but would never look at me. His head was always down. And I thought: 'Well, that head looks sort of familiar,' but I couldn't place him at all, because I didn't see his face. This happened two or three times and then one day he came in and his face was up and I thought: 'My God.' It was my interrogator in Paris in 1942, the one who told me on Xmas Eve '42, that I'd be shot as a spy . . .

As soon as the other interrogators knew about this, they said: 'You can do anything you want with him, take him out and shoot him. We'll close the camp, there's a Tommy gun.' Of course I didn't because I figured I was free and he was locked up.

Stonehouse felt that to have taken the opportunity to kill his former interrogator would have reduced him to the same level as the Gestapo thug.

Vera Atkins felt no sense of satisfaction when sentence was passed at the end of the Natzweiler trial:

I would never have done this job in order to bring these prople to justice. My mind doesn't work like that. I'm afraid I have my own views on the impossibility of meting out justice.

I think that justice is administered according to laws and rules which are laid down and it is the job of the judges and the juries to sort this out, according to the limits within which they work. But whether this is justice or not, I do not know.

I can only say that I have never rejoiced in justice being meted out, necessary though it is. One works very hard to bring people to justice, yes, but administering of justice is someone else's job.

Prince Galitzine returned to civilian life with a deep sense of dissatisfaction. As a young and impressionable man he had seen much horror in so short a time that he remained highly critical of the official attitude:

In fact I thought that we were being far too soft and I still do actually. I think that a lot of the people that were caught by any of those war crimes teams in Europe had committed the most terrible crimes, and we couldn't understand why they were given a year, four years', six years' imprisonment. Very few of them got life and it was really a question of getting either a short term of imprisonment or being hung.

If really one feels that war crimes are a crime against humanity then I think the death penalty should have been inflicted and a lot of us were very surprised at the leniency shown.

The derisory sentences, he felt, were not due to a sense of justice:

I think that there was a natural reaction against killing and against all the horrors of war. And I think because the British nature is forgiving and tolerant there was a feeling among the judges that having caught the people, having actually indicted them and having imprisoned them, that they would – when they got back to their own country – be branded as marked men and therefore they would never be able to live it down.

Time has shown, however, that the culprits did live it down, rapidly re-emerging into public life in Germany.

Epilogue

Had it not been for the Allied planners' decision to mount Operation Loyton, the tide of war would have washed over Moussey and the adjacent communities. As it was they suffered martyrdom for the cause of freedom and Moussey deserves to be ranked with Oradour and Lidice in the list of towns where atrocities were carried out against civilian populations.

A year after the deportations, in September 1945, the SAS returned to Moussey when their dead were given a proper funeral service. The Abbé Gassmann conducted a Roman Catholic requiem mass in the little church, which was followed by the Anglican service for the Burial of the Dead conducted by the Regimental Chaplain, the Rev. John Kent. In view of the problems of maintaining such an isolated cemetery, the Imperial War Graves Commission wanted to remove the bodies to one of their large sites, but the villagers refused to permit 'their boys' to be shifted. To this day they remain buried in that isolated corner of Alsace, their graves still held in honour and decked with flowers.

As far as the SAS is concerned, Moussey is part of their history. The regiment returned there in November 1979 to honour their dead and in memory of the villagers who did not return – in the company of Roger Souchal and the Abbé Molière. Now aged eighty-nine, Molière won the Medaille Militaire at Verdun in 1916. He still tends the graves, does his duties as a priest and once a year wears his red beret with pride. On the last Sunday in September every year the village remembers. After a service in the church, wreaths are laid on the SAS graves and then at the town memorial. A survivor reads out the long list of names and, after each one, another survivor says quietly, 'Mort pour la France'.

Of the participants in this story whose paths crossed for a short time so long ago, all have their memories.

Bill Barkworth emigrated to Australia, married and set up in business. He died of a heart attack in January 1986.

Fred Rhodes returned to Barnsley after 1948 and to his job with the council in the parks department from which he has recently retired. Until approached to take part in *The Secret Hunters* he had not spoken to anyone, including his family, of his role in the War Crimes Investigation Team. In 1985 he returned to Moussey and laid wreaths on behalf of his comrades. He found La Grande Fosse and, in that lonely and forgotten place, left a simple black cross bearing the inscription: 'At this place, eight members of 2nd SAS Regiment were murdered on 15 October 1944.'

Brian Stonehouse has built a career as a highly successful painter.

Odette Churchill, who became Odette Hallowes, was awarded the GC.

Pat O'Leary was awarded the GC and the DSO. He lives in retirement at Waterloo, near Brussels, still better known by his assumed name than as Albert Guerisse. He is President of the International Dachau Committee.

Gerald Draper went on to achieve international respect as an academic lawyer specialising in the field of war criminality and is still in demand all over the world as a lecturer.

Harry Schweiger remained an officer in the army of his adopted country but is still in many ways an Austrian living in Buckinghamshire.

Vera Atkins lives in retirement on the Sussex coast. She is bitter that so little was done in memory of those who died in the camps and that it was left to private enterprise to set up a memorial to the Natzweiler victims. 'We,' she says, 'do less than any other nation to commemorate our people.'

Prince Galitzine runs a public relations consultancy in London. More than forty years have passed since his experience of the horrors of war as a young officer. He commented, 'Time is a great mellower,' and added:

I'd had a lot of very scarring experiences and one was inclined to be rather wholesale perhaps in one's judgments. I was. I didn't recognise the difference between Germans – to me all Germans were cruel, and as a result I was very vengeful.

For many years I just could not bear to be in the same room with a German and it made me absolutely shake. But then after forty years one learns that there are lots of different facets to a nation. I've got a lot of very good German friends. I've gradually got to know them and to respect them. I admit, most of the Germans that I know have been born after 1939. And to them it's another world, and we never talk about those sort of things.

But, at the back of my mind, I shall never forget what happened before and I think that it was very important that we did look for these people. I think it was very important that they were brought to justice, and I think it's very important too that young people of this generation and of the next generation know what happened. Because it could happen again...

Appendices

Appendix A

Statistics at Struthof-Natzweiler

In the early days the Germans registered the deaths of their victims at the Mairie of Natzweiler, the nearest village. Here too can be found the signatures of the doctors responsible. Most of the causes of death are given as 'weak heart', 'heart failure', 'dysentry', or 'typhus'. Only two cases are noted as executed:

> Vladimir Koslow of Krasnodar, peasant
> 'shot by order of the Reichsfuhrer SS'.
> signed: Dr. Max Blancke   13 Jan 43
>
> Gregorj Sterljaschnikow of Jaroslaw
> 'hung'
> signed: Dr. Elmar Precht   2 Jan 43.

The details of the death certificates to be found in the records are as follows:

1941	36 dead
1942	380 dead
1943 (1 Jan/1 Feb)	53 dead

It is improbable that all deaths were listed during this period. In Feb 43 the new crematorium was finished and all registration of deaths was done at the camp. It is estimated that between 5000 and 6000 were killed here, although French reports *(quite unsubstantiated)* put the figure as high as 11,000.

Escape
There are only two known attempts at escape from this camp which have succeeded. The first was in 1941 when the son of a Russian general aided by three of his compatriots seized a German staff car

standing outside the Struthof hotel and got away. Three of the escapees were recaptured and shot. But the Russian general's son is reputed to have got to Switzerland.

During the evacuation of the camp in Sept 44, as the last lorry was leaving the camp, it broke down on the hill outside. With the aid of the local FFI (M. Ernst Krenzer, M. Herry, M. Nicole) four Luxemburgers managed to escape. They have since returned to Luxembourg.

The Germans were very strict during attempts at escape. All prisoners were stood to attention until the man was recaptured, or working parties were made to lie flat with their face on the ground, immobile. In fog the SS guards were most afraid and herded the prisoners together and put them back in their huts.

Evacuation

The camp was evacuated on 4 Sept 44 two months before the arrival of Allied troops and all the prisoners except a cleaning-up party of about 40 were sent back across the Rhine.

The factory was kept in operation by the use of local hired civilian labour.

A Prisoner's Appreciation

A German Communist who had done ten years in various concentration camps told M. Nicole, a foreman, that 'I preferred *Dachau* to this. It is larger so that you can get lost easier; it is better organized and the climate is better.'

Note. The canteen books of the camp giving a fairly complete list of the prisoners' names and numbers were handed to G-I branch Hq 7th Army on 30 Dec 44.

Y. GALITZINE Capt.

Appendix B

German war criminals in the Struthof affair

BLANCKE Dr Max
von BODMANN Dr SS Obersturmfuhrer
BUTTNER, SS Oberschafuhrer of Freiburg
DILLMAN SS Obersturmfuhrer
DREHER SS Oberschafturer
EISELE Dr Hans. Married, born 13 March 1912 at Donau-
  Eschlingen, lives at Weimar, Oberartzt. in SS
EHRMANNTRAUT SS Unterschafuhrer
FUCHS SS Unterschafuhrer of Kehl (Baden)
GRELLACK SS Rottenfuhrer
HAGEN Professor (late of the Medical faculty of Strasbourg)
HEIDER SS Untersturmfuhrer
JUNG Professor of Anatomy (from STRASBOURG)
KRAMER SS Hauptsturmfuhrer. Commandant of the Camp and
  so directly responsible for every crime.
LETZ Dr
NIETSCH SS Oberschafuhrer
OHLER SS Rottenfuhrer
PRECHT Dr Elmar
RUHL Dr
Van MARCKE Belgian architect?
VOLKMAR SS Untersturmfuhrer
WEITZIG SS Oberschafuhrer from Bavaria
ZEUSS SS Hauptschafuhrer and his brother both from Munich

Appendix C

Witnesses for crimes committed at Struthof Camp

1. M. Ernst KRENZER:
Civil engineer at *Rothau*, forced by Germans to work at stone quarries and then to draw up plans for construction of camp.

Worked for intelligence section of FFI. Had continuous access to camp information.

Objective and reliable information.

2. M. NICOLE:
Foreman employed by the firm of stonemasons, contracted by the Germans to supervise quarry work.

Lives at *Rothau*. Employed at camp since the beginning. Also member of FFI.

Information objective and reliable, though lack of education to be considered, because not consistant in report.

3. M. Leon HERRY:
Lives at *Rothau*. Was responsible for the escape and hiding of the four Luxembourgers who are the only prisoners known to have got out.

4. M. Jules ANSTEDT:
Was employed at camp as electrician. Can be contacted through '*Arpocaz*', wine merchant at *Strasbourg*.

Reliability unknown.

5. M. STADLER:
Head of stonemasonry firm from *Grendelbruch*.

Employed in road and quarry work.

Information objective and reliable.

6. M. STEINER:

Mayor of *Natzweiler* – was responsible for issuing the death certificates of the first prisoners killed.

Can give information on identity of many Germans through his official contacts.

Possesses some 500 death certificates signed by camp doctors.

7. Pastor HERRING:

The pastor of *Neuviller*. Helped to pass food and parcels to prisoners.

Information objective and reliable.

8. Johann ERHARDT:

Soldier in SS, a German from the *Banat, Yugoslavia*. Ex-camp guard, deserted to *Natzweiler*. Last heard of in Dec., in the town hall.

Poorly educated but has very valuable information and is willing to talk.

9. M. DANNES:

Lawyer. Works at town hall, *Strasbourg*. Krenzer got him into camp in Aug. 44 to try to rescue General Frere, but was too late. The experience went to his head and his information is inaccurate and unreliable.

10. M. WASSER:

Baker at *Rothau*. Not interviewed.

Reliability unknown.

11. M. JAEGER:

Druggist on *Route du Polygone* (near the post-office)

12. M. HIEGEL:

At *Neudorf*. Not intelligent, reliability unknown.

13. M. George KRIEPER:

FFI officer from *Rothau* district.

Not intelligent. Reliability unknown.

14. M. STAHL:
At police bureau *Strasbourg*. Ex-chief of FFI arrest section.
Interesting as source of further contacts but personally inaccurate
and inconsistant.

15. Four Luxembourgers escaped. (See Appendix D)

Appendix D

Statement made by four witnesses to crimes committed at Struthof-Natzweiler concentration camp

PWB-CPT-Hq. 7th Army
Special Report by Capt. Galitzine.

24 December 1944

SUBJECT: Report signed by Freismuth, Barbel, Schilling and Adam, former inmates of K.Z. Natzweiler (Alsace). English translation.

Following is the translation of a statement made by four members of the Luxemburg resistance movement. Their individual history forms part of the report:

REPORT
by

Josef Freismuth　　Born on 11 Sept. 1914 in Nospelt, Luxembourg. arrested by the gestapo at Esch z/Alzett on 23 Oct. 1942 in Differdingen, Luxemb. on charges of intent to commit high treason and participation in the general strike of 1 Sept. '42.

23 Oct. 32 to 25 Oct. 42, held for investigation at Esch.

26 Oct 42 to 20 Jan. 43 in SS Special Camp at Hinzert (Rhineland).

21 Jan. 43 to 22 Nov. 44 in K Z at Natzweiler, Alsace.

Freed with help of the FFI of Rotau during evacuation of the camp on 22 Nov. 44.

Address: Differdingen, Luxemb., 91 Dicksletzstrasse.

Mathias Barbel	Born on 11 June 1923 in Berdorf, Luxemb. arrested on 2 May 1942 in cityof Luxembourg for rendering assistance to Luxembourg resistance movement, by Luxembourg gestapo 2 May to 30 Jan. 43 in Special SS Camp at Hinzert 31 Jan 43 to 22 Nov. 44, In KZ Natzweiler, Alsace Freed with help of the Rotau FFI during evacuation of the camp on 22 Nov. 44 (Harry, Leon) Address: Bersdorf, Luxembourg or Mme. Schmitt-Barbel Liebfrauenstrasse 32, Luxembourg City.

Adam Konrad	Born on 23 July 1914 in Beauford, Luxembg. arrested on 22 June 42 in Beauford interned until 24 June 42 at Luxembourg then at Hinzert from 24 June 42 to 20 Jan. 43 from 20 Jan 43 to 22 Nov. 44 in KZ Natzweiler, Alsace arrested by the Gestapo of Luxembourg for assistance to the Luxembg. resistance movement. Freed by the Rotau FFI during evacuation of the camp on 22 Nov. 44 Address: Adam Konrad, Beauford, Luxembourg

Leopold Schilling	Born on 11 May 1918 in Beauford, Luxembourg arrested on 22 June 42 at Beauford interned until 24 June 42 in Luxembg. then Hinzert from 24 June 42 to 20 Jan. 43 from 20 Jan. 43 to 22 Nov. 44 in KZ Natzweiler arrested by the Gestapo, Luxembourg for rendering assistance to the Luxembourg resistance movement Freed by the Rotau FFI during evacuation of the camp Address: Schilling, Leopold, Beauford, Luxembourg.

1. *Gas Poisonings*

On 2 Aug. 1943, 59 men and 29 Jewish girls were transferred from the Ravensburg camp to the KZ Natzweiler. Then on 11 Aug., after 8 days of medical examination, 15 women were led to the gas chamber. Upon their death, they were taken to Strasbourg for post-mortem examination. On 13 Aug. the remaining women were killed in the same manner. The first 30 men were killed in this fashion on 17 Aug, the remainder 2 days later.

One of the girls managed to tear herself loose and jumped over a small wall. She was shot dead on the spot.

The following SS-men were responsible for this act:

SS- Hauptsturmfuehrer Kramer (Lagerkommandant)
SS- Obersturmfuehrer Dillmann
SS- Obersturmfuehrer Dr. V. Bodmann
SS- Untersturmfuehrer Volkmar
SS- Oberscharfuehrer Dreher
SS- Rottenfuehrer Grellack

The following morning the undersigned observed blood traces leading from the gas chamber to the loading ramp.

To supplement the aforesaid, may it be added that gas experiments were made from time to time with prisoners, to experiment with new gases, in the course of which, most of them died.

Those responsible for this act are:

Profesor HAGEN of the medical faculty, University of
Strasbourg, as well as his secretary; the two assistants:
Dr. Letz
Dr. Ruhl.

The gas chamber is located outside the camp, in an annex of the Hotel Struthof.

2. *Mutiny in the Quarry* (June 43)

100 Russians and Poles were alleged to have had the intention to prepare a mass escape by overpowering the guards, then seize their weapons and make a get-away. The trial began in the evening toward 9 o'clock, when the alleged ring-leaders were brought up for interrogation; since the investigation chamber was separated from the sleeping quarters by only a thin wooden partition, the other prisoners were able to follow the whole interrogation. In order to extract confessions from the prisoners, their hands were chained to their backs, and they were then strung to the ceiling by their tied

hands. In the course of this, the SS-men participating in the inter-rogation also whipped them. After half an hour was up every single one (of the prisoners) was willing to confess everything the SS-men wanted to know, just to be relieved from their tortures. A few among them lost their minds through their tortures, and began to sing. About 30 were subjected to this torture. The SS-men conduct-ing the interrogation were given wine and spirits to whip-up their fury still further, and afterwards, knew no restraints. The prisoners in the next room could not sleep during the night because of the continuous cries of pain of those being tortured.

At reveille, the accused were taken away. Most of them had been tortured to such an extent that they could no longer walk, but had to be dragged. There were some among them whose faces were bruised so badly that they were entirely beyond recognition. After four weeks, during which time they continued to have their hands tied to their backs and were exposed to the weather, those con-cerned were publicly hung, in the presence of all the prisoners. Those chained in this manner had remained chained at all times, and their hands were not free when they had to relieve themselves, or to eat and drink. The chains grew into their flesh, the upper arms were blue from the stopped blood, and had (so to speak) died off.

The ones responsible for this act were:

SS- Hauptsturmfuehrer Kramer
SS- Oberscharfuehrer Buttner
SS- Hauptscharfuehrer Zeuss
SS- Oberscharfuehrer Nietsch
SS- Unterscharfuehrer Ehrmanntraut
SS- Unterscharfuehrer Fusch
SS- Rottenfuehrer Ohler

3. *Solitary Confinement*

Before the organization of a cell system, all prisoners to be punished were locked up in one cell, 2 meters long and 1.50 meter wide, furnished with one wooden cot. Their hands were chained behind their backs. Food consisted of water and 350 grams of dried bread, and 1 litre of watery soup every three days.

4. *French Prisoners*

In the summer of 1943 the first shipment of French NN-prisoners arrived and it was intended to exterminate them without exception.

On the first Sunday morning of their stay in the camp, they had to fall out in the pouring rain to carry stones from the commandant's building into the camp, in double time, and in so doing they were beaten with sticks by the Blockfuehrers and chased by the dogs until they broke down, completely exhausted. They were then left to lie on the camp parade grounds until noon. Most of them were bleeding profusely from the dog-bites and the slashes of the sticks.

The fifty men concerned were organized into a special work detail, and had to perform the heaviest types of labor in camp. Some of them were put into an extra detail which the prisoners called the 'death detail'. After 14 days, only 30 of the 50 men were still alive. All of them had to work under the worst mistreatment, and were guarded by a chain of sentries. The detail leader, permitted himself the sly joke of sending 2 or 3 prisoners through the sentry line in order to fetch some stones. While doing so, they were shot down by the sentries.

Detail Leader: SS- Unterscharfuehrer Fuchs.

5. *Treatment of NN-prisoners*
Admission to the infirmary was barred to these prisoners. We have seen their wounds which they bandaged with old rags. Those unable to work were dragged to their place of work and left to lie there in the sun or rain all day. They never received hot meals, because they were incapable of work. Their nourishment consisted only of bread. The treatment of the NN-prisoners was such that after a few weeks they were completely exhausted. The term NN-prisoners is applied to people who are guilty of an infraction committed in 'Nacht und Nebel' (night and fog). These people were not allowed to receive mail or personal packages.

6. *Executions*
Only the smallest number of executions were performed according to regulations. The prisoners were killed through a shot in the neck by the SS-men. The SS-men concerned were:

SS- Unterscharfuehrer Fuchs, from Kehl
SS- Unterscharfuehrer Ehrmannstraut, Saarbruecken
SS- Sturmmann Scheuermann

The execution premium consisted of 2×10 litre 'schnaps', 300 grams of sausage, and 6 cigarettes.

In this manner, by hanging and shooting in the neck, 92 women and approximately 300 men were killed during the night of 1st to 2nd Sept. 1944. The corpses were stacked up in a cellar, in which the blood was 20 cm. high. Since these prisoners were not included in the K.Z.N. list, their exact number cannot be stated. They are alleged to be a group of partisans who had been captured in the vicinity.

Those who participated in the above act are:
- SS- Sturmbannfuehrer Hartjenstein
- SS- Obersturmfuehrer Ganninger
- SS- Obersturmfuehrer Dr. Rohde
- SS- Hauptsturmfuehrer Dr. Aus-DemBruch
- SS- Hauptscharfuehrer Zeuss
- SS- Hauptscharfuehrer Straub
- SS- Hauptscharfuehrer Bergemann
- SS- Oberscharfuehrer Hartmann

Still more SS-men probably participated, but we cannot give any names, since nobody was permitted to leave the cell-block during the execution.

During the months of July, August and in the beginning of September, executions by shooting and hanging were carried out almost daily. Only in the rarest cases were executions carried out in front of the prisoners. They mostly were executions of prisoners who had intended to escape. In such cases they were hanged in the presence of the other prisoners, as an intimidation.

The punishment of thrashing was often ordered for minor infractions. Prisoners were laid across a block, and then received 20 to 30 blows on the buttocks, executed with full force.

There have been cases, where a fugitive was recaptured. Then he received more than 100 slashings with a stick or whip so that his buttocks were so badly bruised that for weeks he could neither sit nor lie down. In the case of a thrashing, the whole camp had to assemble. When it was noticed that someone had escaped, the entire camp had to stand in the open until the fugitive had been caught.

7. *Rations Issued*
Much of the blame for the bad state of health of the prisoners can be ascribed to the fact that the food rations to which they were entitled, were subject to embezzlement. They were entitled to the following ration per day:

350 grams bread
25 grams margarine
15 grams meat scraps
50 grams jam (once a week)
20 grams sausage
50 grams cheese (once a week)

Because of embezzlement by those responsible for the provisions, prisoners did not receive the above ration allowances.

The responsibility for this lies with:

SS- Oberscherfuehrer Dreher, from Kaslach, Schwarzwald.

SS- Unterschurfuehrer Becker, Saarlautern.

Most of the time the noon-meal soup consisted of turnips with two to three unpeeled potatoes.

The above is not meant as a complete report, but only as extracts of the most important subject matter.

Signed by: Barbel, Freismuth, Schilling, Adam. . . .

YURKA N. GALITZINE
Capt.

Appendix E

List of accused and suspect accused, with location where known

Hstut.	**ALBRECHT**
	ARNOLD Albert
	BERG Franz
	BERGER Rudi
	Bobby (? van HOUT)
Hptm.	**BOHNEN**
Ostuf.	**BRAUN**
Stuscha.	**BRONNER**
Oscha.	**BRÜckle** Georg
Hstuf.	**BUCK** Karl
Uscha.	**BUSCH** Hans
	Charlie (? CAMBA)
	CHAVANNE Paul
Oscha.	**DIETRICH** Heinrich
	DINKEL
Ostuf.	**EISENMENGER** Walter
Stubaf.	**ERNST** Hans Dieter Dr.
	FAURE Jeannot
Oscha.	? Fernand
Stuscha.	? Franz
Uscha.	**FUCHS** Peter
Hscha.	**FISCHER** Karl (Kdo. Schöner)
	FISCHER Willi
Hscha.	**GAEDE** Horst
Ostuf.	**GANNINGER**
Hstuf.	**GEHRUM** Julius
Uscha.	**GEIGER** August
Hscha.	**GIEGLING** Kurt

114

Hstuf.	GÖLKEL Karl Adam
Hscha.	GRIEM
Ostuf.	GUTH
Ostubaf.	HARTJENSTEIN
Stuscha.	HILKER Heinrich
Ogruf.	HOFFMANN
Uscha.	HOOS
Schar.	HÜBNER Hans
Staf.	ISSELHORST Erich Dr.
	Jean (? LASNIER)
Hscha.	JANTZEN Walter
Uscha.	JUND
Ogruf.	KALTENBRUNNER Dr.
Oscha.	KESTER Max
Stubaf.	KOLB
	LEDRAPPIER Jean
Uscha.	LIEDLOFF Peter Hugo
Schar.	MACHATSCHEK
Hstuf.	MEIER Ernst
Hstuf.	MEYER
Ostuf.	MEYER Emil
Hstuf.	MÖLLER
Gruf.	MÜLLER
Ustuf.	MUNTSCH
Oberw.	MUTH
Uscha.	MUTTERER Rene
Ustuf.	NAGELER Fritz
Oberw.	NEUSCHWANGER Heinrich
Oberltn.	NUSSBERGER Karl
Ogruf.	OBERG
Rttf.	OHLERT
Stuscha.	OPELT Fritz
Stuscha.	ORTSTADT Hans
Meister	OSTERTAG Erwin
	PERDON Louis
Hscha.	PILZ Josef
Ustuf.	PREIL Gerhart
	PRZYBISCHI Henri
Ostubaf.	PULLMER
	RADET Jean

Major	REISSER
	? René
Hstuf.	RETZEK Helmuth
Ostuf.	RHODE Dr.
	SAVRE Robert
General	SEEGERS
Ostubaf.	SUHR
Hstuf.	SCHIELE
Ostuf.	SCHLUDE Hermann
Ostubaf.	SCHNEIDER Wilhelm
Stuscha.	SCHNEIDER Willy
Hscha.	SCHNEIDER Willy
Ostuf.	SCHÖNER Erwin
Stuscha.	SCHOSSIG
Ustuf.	SCHUMANN
Hstuf.	SCHNURR
Stuscha.	STASSIK
Ostubaf.	STINDT Dr.
Hscha.	STRAUB Peter
Stubaf.	UHRING Robert
	ULLRICH Benno
	VARESTE Robert
	VASSEUR Jacque
Ostuf.	VEESE Joachim
Gauleiter	WAGNER Robert
Oscha.	WALDE Hermann
Hstuf.	WENGER Erich
Oscha.	WILDE Erich
Oberst	WOLFF
Ltn.	WOLFF
Ustuf.	WÜNSCH Robert
Uscha.	WUTTKE Willibald
Uscha.	ZÄHRINGER Georg

Appendix F

Letter sent to the citizens of Moussey as a form of thank you for their help

Now that the war with Germany has been victoriously ended, I wish to express to you something of the gratitude which all the officers and men of the Special Air Service Brigade who took part in the campaign of France, 1944, feel towards you for the selfless devotion and memorable courage with which you aided them in the accomplishment of their tasks. The help you gave contributed in a large measure to any success we achieved, and we are full of admiration for the disregard of danger and the generosity of spirit with which that help was given.

All men who were involved in the bitter conflict of 1939-1945 grew to recognise the importance to victory of civilian loyalty, steadfastness and determination. We realise that in no country and at no time did the practise of those virtues demand greater firmness than in France under German occupation, and that nowhere was that firmness more abundantly forthcoming. Your individual acts of patriotism as they affected our operations have been brought to the notice of the British Government and will be preserved in the official records of the British War Office.

Those of our men who had known France before, returned to England with renewed faith in the destiny of your country to which the civilisation of the world owes so much: those who had not known France before have now an impression of a great people of indomitable spirit. All the British troops under my command have been most deeply touched by the sentiments of comradeship with England which their allies of France have expressed to them in words, and so valiantly proved in deeds. It is our fervent hope that the unity of purpose and ideals between Great Britain and France which we have realised in war will be maintained triumphantly in peace.

On behalf of the Special Air Service Brigade, I wish all good fortune to you personally and to France and offer you our most sincere thanks.

(signed) J. M. Calvert, Brigadier
Commander SAS Troops,

June, 1945.   1 British Airborne Corps.

Acknowledgments

During the lengthy period I spent collecting information, a number of people were most generous with their time, the loan of personal documents and photographs, and were prepared to endure my endless questions. I list them not in any particular order of merit and would apologise to any I may have omitted: Miss Vera Atkins, Alan Nightingale, Professor Gerald Draper, Lord Silkin, Lord Elwyn Jones, Rick Moddiman, Captain Harry Schweiger, Walther Freud, Roger Elliott, Fred (Dusty) Rhodes, Brian Stonehouse, 'Pat O'Leary', Fred Warner, Frank Kelly, John Hodge, Prince Yurka Galitzine, Dr Quentin Hughes, Colonel Cleaver, Charles Kaiser, and members of the SAS Regiment.

Thanks are due to The Wiener Library, London, for permission to reproduce the photographs on page 7.

Index